How & When To
SIGN A BOOK DEAL

(Advice to Authors)

Helen Cox is a Yorkshire-born novelist and poet. After completing her MA in creative writing at the University of York St. John Helen wrote for a range of magazines and websites as well as writing news and features for TV and radio. Helen edited her own independent film magazine for five years and has penned several non-fiction books. Her first two novels were published by HarperCollins in 2016. She currently hosts The Poetrygram podcast and coordinates poetry and non-fiction courses at City Lit, London. Helen's new series of cosy mysteries stars librarian-turned-sleuth Kitt Hartley, and is set in Yorkshire.

ADVICE TO AUTHORS SERIES

How to Become a Published Writer

How to Write Page-Turning Fiction

How to Write Sex

How & When To SIGN A BOOK DEAL

(Advice to Authors Series Book 1)

By **Helen Cox**

CONTENTS

DISCLAIMER

Please note, dearest reader, that this book is not intended as legal advice. I never graduated from the Acme School of Law, or any other esteemed legal institution. This volume is written with the intention of supporting authors who are either on the brink of a book deal or intending to enter into one in the future. There are various elements involved when striking the best book deal for you and this guide is designed to help you navigate them, alongside professional advice. Before entering any legally binding contract, please ensure you seek counsel from a lawyer or literary agent.

Signing a literary contract is an important, life-altering business decision that could affect the long-term income you reap from any assets you have created. It is a decision that rests entirely with you. The author cannot be held responsible for any adverse situations that arise during the negotiation of your book deal, or beyond. But, from what I've seen in movies, I can tell you that it's not advisable to make any deals with the devil. Even if they look like Al Pacino or Liz Hurley. It didn't work out well for Keanu Reeves or Brendan Fraser, and I get the distinct feeling it wouldn't work out any better for you.

WHAT'S YOUR
STORY?

——

What's my story? Good question. You're sparky and inquisitive. I like that about you.

Over the last decade I have signed book deals with both fiction and non-fiction publishers. Throughout those ten years I have had experiences within the industry that range from eye-wateringly tragic to downright inspirational. This volume is designed to steer you away from the former and propel you towards the latter by, to put it eloquently, saving you from making the same big dumb mistakes I made when I first started working with publishing houses.

Alongside my work with traditional publishing houses, I've also self-published various books, pamphlets and anthologies. This means I can offer you some insight into the realities of independent publishing which is just one alternative to signing with a traditional publisher.

My publishing career officially started back in 2010 when I masochistically decided to independently publish a film magazine. I edited and produced New Empress Magazine for five years (sharp learning curve, ahoy!). In that time I also self-published two non-fiction books and had my first non-fiction paperback traditionally published.

By 2016 I had secured a fiction contract with Harper Collins for two New York-set romance novels and by the end of 2018 I secured a three book deal — later extended to a six book deal — with Quercus Books.

In between writing a Yorkshire-set murder mystery series featuring a crime-solving librarian, I self-publish non-fiction books like this one. I like to pay it forward whenever I can, and producing writing guides is one of the ways I do that.

For years there was no term for an author with both traditional publishing and self-publishing experience. I heard a whisper that a group of wizened writers who formed a not-so-secret esoteric coven actually held a séance in an attempt to get in touch with Homer, believing he would have the answer. I humbly suggested that 'Publishing Halfling' might be a good term, but this buzz word never took off despite numerous social media campaigns. Ultimately, some anonymous industry forerunner decided one idle Thursday afternoon to call us 'hybrid authors.'

This term is not quite as epic as Publishing Halfling in my opinion but I've made my peace with it.

Hybrid authors have the benefit of knowing the plus and minus factors for working in both halves of the publishing arena, and this book is designed to offer some insight into whether you'd be happier all round as an indie publisher, whether you'd prefer to sign-up with a traditional publisher or whether you'd be prudent to do a bit of both if possible.

Book deals are touted as the most desirable prize an author can win, and don't get me wrong, I'm incredibly grateful to my publishers for the continuous work they do in ensuring my books reach the widest possible audience. But a book deal is a very strange beast. It has downy Labrador ears but teeth where you don't expect them. It is both a deeply personal experience and a professional agreement. Consequently, signing a traditional publishing contract won't be the right choice for everyone. In writing this book I hope to save authors, and any editors or publishing professionals they may work with, some unnecessary heartache by offering strategies you can use to make sure the deal on the table is the right one for you before you sign on the dotted line. I also offer advice in making sure the relationship between you and any publisher you choose to sign with is as fruitful and positive as possible.

PART 1:

How to
ATTRACT A PUBLISHER
—

Anyone who has dutifully read most of the information out there about landing a publishing deal may wonder why this chapter of the book even exists. Surely, there is only one way to attract a publisher: have a really fantastic book to sell. *Dammit Helen, why are you wasting our time? I hear you cry.*

Although ten to fifteen years ago the advice may have focused on a gleaming manuscript in which nary a comma is out of place, the publishing industry has metamorphosed in that time from a hidden oubliette to a courtly banquet where almost anyone can find room at the table if they have a saleable product. Thus, there are many ways of making yourself a more attractive prospect to a traditional publisher if that is your heart's desire.

The first step on the quest to a traditional book deal is to work out what kind of book you've written or are writing. Broadly speaking, fiction books can be separated into two main categories: literary and genre fiction. Genre fiction is anything that fits into a clear, er, well, genre such as horror, romance or science-fiction. Literary fiction often defies traditional genre categories and instead tends to focus on internal struggle, enlightenment and tragedy.

In addition to fiction genres you also have non-fiction and poetry — all of which have their own subcategories.

Nobody is going to cross your palm with gold, however, if they don't know what goods they are buying. That means you need to be clearer than river water straight from the source about what kind of book you're trying to get publishers, and by proxy agents, interested in. Your approach will differ somewhat depending on what kind of book you're writing. So gather round, brave ones, and heed the wisdom of this publishing crone. I will show you some possible paths through the woods.

ADVICE TO GENRE FICTION AUTHORS

> *"I've been as bad an influence on American literature as anyone I can think of."* **— Dashiell Hammett**

Greetings, my much-maligned friends of the genre fiction fold. This portion of the book is written just for you. If our reputations are to be believed we are the cads of the fiction world; an unrelenting bad influence on the impressionable minds of gentle readers. Why then, you may rightfully ask, do the likes of us keep getting published?

THE ANSWER IS: MONEY.

Bookshop owners may never stand your book next to those of lofty award-winners, but they know and publishers know that, if it's packaged right, your book has a good chance of becoming a cash cow that will help them keep the lights on for the next six months. Still, given its mass appeal, there are lots of people out there submitting genre fiction manuscripts. So how do you make sure yours is the one that publishers say 'yes' to?

If your manuscript falls into a specific subgenre, your first task is to seek out other successful books in the same genre. Once you've done that, you can write a sales pitch to an agent (or editor who accepts open submissions) in which you explain how your book appeals to readers of those books and how the book will pleasantly surprise readers in the genre. Some of the most successful genre books out there take what has gone before as a template and twist it for effect.

A good example of this is the thriller genre where writers are challenged with coming up with a twist readers will never see coming. Because the genre has been around for a while *(The Count of Monte Christo* published in 1844 is cited as an early example), the twists have become more and more elaborate in order to surprise and delight readers.

In your missive to any publisher or agent, you must be transparent about how your manuscript builds on what readers enjoy about the genre and in which ways the story manipulates those traditional tropes to offer those who buy your book a fresh reading experience. Essentially, you are trying to pinpoint a very specific target audience and explain how you will serve them. If it helps, think of yourself as an ancient mythical archer who is trying to hit a target. If you miss it means death... or, you know, the author equivalent: a rejection letter.

If it doesn't help to imagine yourself as an ancient mythical archer then please don't. Just know that the worst thing you can write in a letter to an agent is 'my book appeals to everyone' even if that happens to be true, it's not what agents and publishers need or want to hear. They need to know how to pigeonhole you, package and promote you, in less than a minute. They don't mean to be rude, but they are busy people.

Another tactic commercial fiction authors can use to attract a traditional publisher is to pitch the book they've written as the first in a series. Ideally, you will have written more than one instalment in the series already — or at least have started the next book. Commercial fiction editors are generally keener on series these days because, in the Western world at least, we have developed a binge culture (thank you Netflix... or possibly Pringles. It's difficult to say exactly who started it). That is, when people find something they enjoy, they want as many instalments of it as they can get as soon as they can get them. Thus, it's highly likely that if you write a genre series your publisher will want to work to a rapid release schedule, releasing a book every few months. With this in mind, whether you write historical romance or high fantasy, it's prudent to have at least the first two books written before you even query an agent. If I had my time over again I'd have three books written in advance.

As it was, I sent the first manuscript I ever wrote off to a publisher. It was accepted and I've been trying to catch-up ever since. I'm not complaining about having my first ever fiction manuscript accepted for publication. Who would do that? But I am saying I could have played it smarter if I wasn't naïve, impatient and generally blundering. And as we've already established in the introductory chapter, you, dear reader, are going to be much smarter about this than I ever was. If there are awards out there for being the best at navigating the world of publishing unscathed, you are going to be at least nominated for them by the time we're done here.

Other than the binge culture factor, publishers also know that they can make a much better return on investment on a series of books than they can on a standalone book. Now, this is a huge generalization. Naturally, there will always be those huge breakaway books that for some reason become massive bestsellers and nobody really knows why, but everyone buys a copy. There is a chance that you have written that book, but a publisher has little chance of knowing you've written that book just by reading the manuscript. If they knew which books would be huge breakaway hits they would only publish huge breakaway hits. Thus, it makes sense to give your publisher and agent as many reasons to say 'yes' to you as possible, and writing a series is definitely a tick in the plus column for most people who represent and publish genre fiction.

If you don't want to write a series then, at the very least, commit to a chosen genre. Moreover, when you query agents and publishers, that is the time to profess your undying love for the genre you're currently writing in. Commitment phobes will not fare well here — you have been warned. So, deep down inside, you may know you don't want to write in this genre until your dying day. And secretly, you've always wanted to have a go at writing a romantic space-opera about a time-travelling pirate... wait... is that just me? But your agent and editor don't need to know this on a first meeting. For now it is best to pledge your commitment to your chosen genre and explain that you expect to be writing stories in this category for the foreseeable future.

This is important because the agent and the publisher will want confidence that they can build your 'brand' as an author. Given the amount of time they will put in to getting your book made and out there in the world, this is a fair request. Most authors progress to different genres in the long-term but it tends to stay pretty static in the beginning. Stephen King, for example, was known for writing horror and, to a certain extent, still is. Danielle Steele is known for romances. Lee Childs is known for thrillers. These author names are, up to a point, synonymous with their genre. People hear their name and know what kind of book to expect. That's exactly the effect your publisher will be hoping to create for you. But in order to do it they need to know that you are in for the long haul.

The last nugget of sage wisdom I'm going to bestow, fellow genre authors who wish to attract a publisher, is to build some kind of platform that gives you access to readers in your genre. Do you have a mailing list where you discuss the genre? Did you set up a Facebook Group? An Instagram page? A website forum? Something that gives you the opportunity to interact with your target readership? There have been people who have been approached by publishers on the basis of their Instagram following alone. So don't underestimate just how desirable a platform is. There is a good chance that any agent or publisher that makes an offer has looked you up online first to see what kind of online presence you have. Why not save them the trouble and mention how many subscribers you have in your query letter? By explaining how many readers you have direct access to already, before you've even signed a contract, you're giving a publisher another reason to say 'yes' to your manuscript.

More advice on publishing and creating a strong manuscript can be found in the free creative writing starter library offered through my mailing list:

helencoxbooks.com/writerscommunitylist.

Advice to Literary Authors

As I have spent my fiction career writing commercial fiction, my advice in this section is based on discussions I've had with the many literary authors I have known and worked with over my time in the industry. For you, the route into publishing probably hasn't changed quite as much in the last ten years. This doesn't mean that you still don't have options or that you can't find ways of making your manuscript seem more attractive to a publisher, but it does mean that you are more likely to be catapulted into the spotlight by following more traditional guidelines.

If you bypassed the advice to genre authors section because you already know that you are a lofty literary artiste, please go back and take a look at what I've written there. Most of it, save my strange if brief tangent about time-travelling pirates, is still of relevance to you. Just as genre fiction authors are advised to conduct research on who is striking it rich in their category right now, it is prudent for literary authors to get a handle on which literary titles have done well in recent years. Moreover, it's useful to find out what readers of literary fiction tend to be drawn to in terms of setting, themes and character.

It's also not going to harm your chances of getting published traditionally if you build a platform. In fact this increases the likelihood of you achieving what so many literary writers sadly fail to achieve: make a living off your books alone. A literary novelist is, on the whole, likely to sell fewer books than a genre novelist because their work doesn't have the same mass appeal. Commercial fiction writer Mickey Spillane probably said it best when he defended his 'low-brow' work with the following statement: "*Those big-shot writers could never dig the fact that there are more salted peanuts consumed than caviar.*"

Of course, just because you're not necessarily going to make money from your books, doesn't mean you shouldn't write them. Above all, I think you should write what you enjoy and what's in your heart. I'm sentimental that way. However, this is a business-orientated book for writers and consequently, I want to prepare you for the fact that literary writers are known for bemoaning the low income yielded from their books. It's unfair of course. Literary authors write the great books of our time. Books that have the capacity to hold a mirror up to our society or genuinely change the way we behave towards others for the better. And they don't see a lot of money for it.

Still, the trade-off is that literary authors do get all the prestige. I am unlikely to win any awards for my time-travelling pirate space-opera, and when I sit next to strangers at weddings and tell them I write books, they will ask me what kind and I will say time-travelling pirate space operas, they will look down their noses at me and there will be nothing I can do about it, except down another glass of prosecco.

But you, cunning wordsmith of articulate and important works, they will be fascinated by you. They will tell their children and grandchildren that they once sat next to you at a friend's wedding. They will ask you lots of insightful questions about your process and tell you they read about your book in *The Sunday Times*. I'm still not convinced that money and prestige are a fair exchange for you, but currently that's the way the market stands.

I should point out here — in case you are suddenly rethinking the Great American Novel you started last week — that even though you might not make as much from book sales, there are other sources of income for the literary greats including teaching, awards money, payment for literary short stories and panel events. That said, there are no guarantees that these things will be extended to you and thus it makes sense to exploit every possible avenue of raising your profile as a writer. Making sure you have a decent website and a mailing list — preferably with thousands of subscribers who are hungrily following your writing journey — will certainly help. I'm sure any publisher would be pleased to hear that you'd already made a start on these things before your book has even secured a publishing deal.

On the whole though, the main method of securing a traditional fiction contract for a literary author is to write short stories that either appear in reputable journals and magazines or are shortlisted for reputable contests. I have known literary authors to win just one short story prize and find at least three emails from literary agents land in their inbox over the coming weeks, even if they haven't already finished their novel manuscript. For a commercial fiction writer this kind of event would be pretty much unthinkable but, because of the way the literary route works, if you have the patience to wait for a reputable magazine to say 'yes' to a short story, or to wait for a competition to go through the judging process, then you have a significantly higher chance of luring agents to you rather than having to approach them. I know that seems quite a radical thought. We're taught to think of agents as shape-shifting pixies who one might only happen to meet every ninety years 'neath the blue light of a lunar eclipse. For years, I didn't believe that agents ever approached authors until I befriended some literary writers and found out they were being courted by numerous agents trying to win their hands.

Naturally, this is unlikely to happen overnight. For one thing, you have to write short fiction to a quality that will be accepted by magazine editors, and you have to do this consistently. For the literary author, the first couple of years of their career largely consists of sending out short works to respectable outlets and writing new stuff whilst they are waiting to hear back from editors. It is a repetitive process which requires persistence and the aforementioned patience (side note: I have zero patience and thus could never have been a literary author. An editor holding onto one of my stories for six months when it could have been out in the world as an ebook or blog post would have been akin to medieval torture for the likes of me). But if you have those qualities, you can definitely make this route work for you.

Even if you don't find three emails from agents in your inbox after the first few publications, after a year or eighteen months, you will be able to send a query letter to an agent with a list of publications in which you have been published, and hopefully a list of competitions and contests in which you have either been shortlisted or have won. You could also raise your literary profile by taking part in literary residencies. This is where institutions pay you a grant to come and write and teach at their venue. Being selected for this kind of opportunity is definitely going to make you stand out from other authors in your query letter. A good place to find such opportunities is the National Association of Writers in Education Website. If you are outside the UK search for literary residencies in your area or approach some local cultural institutions about setting one up. Do you have a museum in your area that would love a pamphlet of flash fiction or poetry inspired by their exhibits? Just because you're a literary author doesn't mean you can't be entrepreneurial.

Perhaps not all of these strategies are a fit for your lifestyle and circumstances. That's OK. Just pick one or two and do your best with them. Your aim is to become a more attractive prospect than the literary author who finished their manuscript last week and has no literary profile of any kind. In the traditional world, literary authors are expected to play the long game.

If you choose the independent publishing route, things will move more quickly for you in some respects, but you will also face an additional challenge when compared to genre authors. Your work doesn't fit into an easily marketable (and searchable) category, which means it's more difficult for readers to find you. There are many literary authors who have successfully self-published their work however, proving these challenges are not insurmountable. If you discover it would be more profitable, or more fitting, to independently publish your book rather than offer it to a traditional publisher, then this is still a valid option. After all, if it's good enough for David Mamet, it's good enough for all of us, right?

Regardless of whether you publish your work traditionally or through the indie route, building a literary profile through magazines, journals and contests will definitely be a big help. It offers readers what's known as 'social proof'. This is essentially evidence that other people have read and enjoyed your work and thus, given the right platform, more people might too. So, if you have just finished your masterpiece, why not get started on letting people know who you are and what you're about? Not only will it pay dividends in time, it will make a pleasant change to talking to your cat.

Not that your cat isn't a formidable conversationalist.

ADVICE TO NON-FICTION AUTHORS

"Writing fiction is fun. Writing non-fiction is life-changing." – **A.D. Posey**

What about those of us who have sworn to tell the truth when we tell stories? Where do we fit into the grand publishing picture? The route into traditional publishing for non-fiction authors will depend greatly on what kind of non-fiction you write. If you have written a memoir or some other kind of autobiographical or biographical piece, it's advisable to look at the advice to commercial and literary fiction authors on previous pages as you will follow a very similar process to them.

If you're writing a non-fiction book about a specific subject, a self-help or how-to guide of some nature, you have numerous options when it comes to getting your book out in the world. You can still approach agents if you are looking to build a long-term literary career. Those that manage non-fiction clients will have guidelines on their website on how to propose a non-fiction volume that they can sell on to a publisher.

A proposal usually consists of three sample chapters, an outline for the rest of the book and an explanation of your credentials and what makes you the person best-placed to write and sell this book with authority. As agents spend their time building relationships with publishers, and because they have a greater sense of what other authors have been offered in the past, they will be able to strike a more favourable deal for you than you would if you went in on your own.

If you are unable to acquire an agent to represent you, it is possible to approach some publishers direct. If you decide on this route, you can give yourself the best chance of acceptance by: following the guidelines on their website to the letter, conducting in-depth market research and building a platform where you can interact with readers on the subject.

If a publisher offers you a direct deal it is imperative you seek legal advice on the contract as you will not have an agent to argue for better terms or make sure that all elements of a contract support your best creative outcomes. The Alliance of Independent Authors offers both legal support and a panel of pro-indie rights agents that would be of help in such circumstances.

Although I wouldn't be without an agent now, I did go into my first ever traditional book deal solo. I started out in this business by self-publishing two non-fiction books that were what would now be referred to as 'books of my heart'. I wrote an alternative film history book about movies everyone else thought were terrible and I then hopped subjects and wrote a local history book about The Tees Transporter Bridge, which is both an example of engineering brilliance and an emblem of regional pride in North Yorkshire where I hail from. Given that both of these projects were extremely personal and niche, I didn't expect them to hold much interest to mainstream publishers, and frankly, I didn't want a large institution rearranging something that was essentially a passion project.

Independently publishing my first two non-fiction volumes worked well for me. It gave me the creative freedom to work on my own terms whilst also teaching me what it really took to finish a book. After building my confidence with these first two volumes — which sold surprisingly well — I then approached The History Press with a proposal for my third book by following the guidelines on their website. This proposal was accepted — it helped that I already had a platform as a magazine editor — and a book was published. I didn't have an agent at that time, so I asked a friend of a friend who worked in publishing what they thought of the terms. They confirmed that the terms were standard as far as non-fiction contracts go.

Satisfied that I wasn't getting a raw deal, and knowing that this book was niche and thus more about developing my writing portfolio than making big money, I didn't quibble the terms. I signed the contract and it did exactly what I expected it to do: it raised my literary profile and made me a bit of pocket money. This was my first experience with traditional publishing and it was a positive one. Not because it made me enough money to retire on or because I became an internationally renowned author as a result, but because the outcome matched my expectations going in. Which, I believe, is the secret to almost every successful business transaction — both parties have expectations and both parties deliver on the expectations of the other.

At the beginning of this book however, I explained that I very much wanted to give you the opportunity to be smarter and savvier than I ever was. With this in mind, I would recommend you hire an experienced lawyer to instruct you on the terms of the contract. This is especially important for those of you who have a book with wide appeal — e.g. books about business or career change — as these kinds of books can be worth a lot of money and may have enough market appeal that you don't need a publisher.

If you have yet to be offered a contract, building a platform in the area you wish to write in is likely going to be the best route to getting a 'yes' to your proposal. Remember, a whole section of the proposal is usually dedicated to an explanation about why you are best placed to write this book. Without an established platform in your area of expertise, writing that portion of the proposal is going to be tougher than scaling Mount Doom.

Non-fiction authors often use a range of different platforms to reach readers before they even think about sending a book proposal out. Blogs, YouTube channels, Facebook groups and, again, trusty mailing lists will help you convince a non-fiction publisher that your book is a sure bet as you will already have begun building a readership around your topic, and when the book is released, you will have a ready-made audience to sell to. This is an invaluable asset for any author when approaching the gargoyled gates of any traditional publishing house without the backing of an agent.

ADVICE TO
POETS

———

"There is no money in poetry, but then there is no poetry in money, either." **– Robert Graves**

Apologies if the following statement is like an Excalibur-stab through the heart but, relatively speaking, there are only a handful of literary agents out there who handle poetry manuscripts. This is because on the whole there is little money to be made from poetry alone. The good news is, like anything, there are exceptions to this rule. In recent years people like Rupi Kaur and Nikita Gill have become internationally renowned and have, hopefully, earnt a decent amount of money from their book sales.

At the time of writing, Rupi Kaur has 3.9 million Instagram followers. Nikita Gill has half a million Instagram followers. Both represent formidable platforms. Rupi Kaur's following was no doubt helped to reach even greater heights than that of Nikita Gill's by Kaur's decision to tour almost every university that would have her in order to build an audience for her work. What I'm saying is: these two poets didn't simply write a collection of poems and then find themselves accidentally shot to poetic superstardom. They both worked hard on building their platform for some time in order to achieve the level of book sales required to reach international fame.

I don't want to give you the impression that nobody represents poets. There are agencies out there that will but, for the most part, you might find yourself feeling a little bit out in the cold. Publishing is, after all, a money-making business and the bulk of market sales don't happen in the poetry section. Consequently, you might find that more doors close in your face than they do for writers of longer works. That said, social media has inspired a resurgence of interest in poetry and there are still many small presses out there interested in publishing pamphlets and collections that you can approach directly. A good place to find out about such opportunities is the National Poetry Library in the UK and the Submittable website worldwide. There, you will find lists of opportunities curated for poets that will save you a lot of sieving through blogs, websites and magazines.

Before you approach a publisher about a collection, it is wise to build a literary profile just as an author writing a longer piece of literary fiction might. With millions of poets to choose from, it is makes sense to ensure you stand out by first submitting individual poems to contests, magazines and journals for publication. If your poetry has been shortlisted for a prize or made it into a list of magazines and journals, the odds are the editor in question will give your work more consideration than a poet who hasn't gone through this process.

In addition to this, just as with genre and literary authorship, you shouldn't underestimate the value of a platform. Do you think it's a coincidence that Rupi Kaur and Nikita Gill happen to have a huge Instagram following and also happen to be published? No. They both had followings which grew even bigger once they were published. The fact that they had a ready-made readership that the publisher could sell books to directly will have made the risks of publishing these poets seem slim and the benefits great.

Only a few poets will reach this magnitude of success, but even so I would like to quibble somewhat with the Robert Graves quote that heads up this section of the book. It's often true that there is no direct money in selling poetry books. I've sold hundreds of independently-published pamphlets and I'm not yet retired, but it would be wrong to say that my poetry doesn't make me any money. Through writing poetry and hosting a poetry podcast, I have had some lucrative doors in the literary world open up to me. People have approached me to teach workshops, give lectures and talk at residential festivals. All of which has paid. All of which has raised my profile. All of which is a direct result of them enjoying my poetry in the numerous magazines, anthologies and journals it has appeared in.

In short, the hard work can and does pay off but often not in the ways you expect it to. For me, writing poetry is all about joy. I don't put it out into the world expecting anything back, so when someone does approach me with an opportunity like those listed above it is always a surprise. A welcome surprise but a surprise nonetheless.

Moreover, just because agents may not be lining up to represent poets, that doesn't mean you're alone. There is a huge community of online poets who share ideas, poems and materials that support others in their craft. Sometimes we also contemplate forming a legion of explorers and going on a quest to uncover the true resting place of the holy grail, but common sense tends to kick in before we actually step foot out of the door. If you're looking for a place to start in terms of finding useful online resources, you can pick up a free poetry polishing masterplan and 100 poetry prompts when you sign up to my writers community mailing list. Visit HelenCoxBooks.Com for more information.

All right, now that we've outlined some solid strategies for ensuring your work is an attractive prospect for a publisher, let's take a look at some next steps in terms of securing a book deal.

WHAT IF I HAVE A QUERYING FAIL?

"The only failure in writing is when you stop doing it. Then you fail yourself." **– Natalie Goldberg**

Readers of this book will likely be at different stages of the querying process. Some may have just finished the first draft of their manuscript, others may have an agent who is in the process of sending out their manuscript to editors, some may have just had interest from a publisher while others may be performing human sacrifices to the intergalactic overlords beneath the full moon. Just kidding, I was only making sure I had your attention because this next part is really important and pretty much applies to all writers at any stage of their career — yes, even published authors can have a querying fail.

If you follow the advice set out in this volume thus far: if you research your market, build your platform, build your literary profile and still have no success in terms of acquiring an agent or publisher, that does not mean you are out of options or that you are 'forced' to publish independently.

To be clear, approaching an agent with your manuscript is the time-honoured manner of acquiring a traditional publishing contract, but you should be aware that some publishers accept direct submissions. Joffe Books, Hera Books and Bookouture are just three examples of publishers who allow you to submit manuscripts via their website. Thus, before you chalk this attempt up to a querying fail just because every agent rejected your manuscript, make sure you've explored all of the direct methods of getting your work on the desk of a commissioning editor too.

All of this advice is based on the understanding that you have your heart set on a traditional contract. That, for whatever reason, a traditional publishing deal is your ultimate life goal. If you have exhausted all avenues with agents and publishers with this manuscript, one way you can keep your eye on the long-term goal is to start your next manuscript while continuing to enter your first manuscript into competitions and contests to see if you can get it shortlisted or perhaps even win a prize.

You could also choose to set up a Patreon page and build a following by posting a chapter every day to fans of the genre. Since Patreon is a private platform it will not count as publishing your work, which gives you the option to resubmit the manuscript six months or a year later. New agents start on the literary scene quite regularly so it is worth waiting a while and trying again. They might take an interest in the story in a way others haven't, especially if it has already had some recognition in competitions or has the following like the one you would build on Patreon.

Additionally, there are online opportunities to pitch your manuscript to agents worldwide via Twitter. The #PitMad challenge is an online pitch party where authors can pitch their polished manuscripts to agents in 280 characters or fewer. Agents follow the hashtag and 'favourite' any pitches for manuscripts they would like to receive.

If you've exhausted all of these suggestions and still don't have any success, then by this point you should have a new manuscript to shop around. If that one gets published, or the one after that, at some point a publisher will ask you if you happen to have anything already written that could be published. Your agent might also ask you if you've got anything sitting in a drawer that could be revised and submitted to editors. You will be amazed by how quickly people will readily accept things that they had previously rejected once you have a proven track record as an author who sells.

The important point to remember is: a 'no' today does not mean no forever, and if a traditional contract is truly what you desire, then with persistence, and a willingness to keep writing until the right manuscript lands on the right desk, it is highly likely that at some point your work will find an editor who believes they can sell it. And when that happens you will have the most incredible origin story to tell. It will be up there with Steve Rogers and Bruce Wayne. People will make you tell it again and again, how you wrote and wrote, how you submitted and submitted until you found the publishing professional who believed in you and your work.

The added bonus is, most people listening to that story will have their own dream of being traditionally published and the fact that you didn't give up on your dream might inspire somebody else not to give up on theirs. Since writers pretty much have to write, because that's the way they process the world, we may as well keep writing and inspire a few people along the way if we can.

Can't My Agent
HANDLE THE DEAL?

—

As stated in my ultra-serious disclaimer, this book is not designed as a substitute for professional advice from an agent or lawyer. If you, like me, are one of those lucky people who has a literary agent, you might be wondering if you even need to read this book. Can't they just handle the deal without you?

Well, they are likely to do a lot of the heavy lifting. For example, there's no doubt that they will be invaluable in making sure the best possible monetary terms are in place and that you don't sign away all of your rights for the length of copyright with no hope of ever getting them back again. Poets acting without an agent should definitely seek legal advice before signing a contract for this very reason. That said, when striking a deal of this nature, there are other elements to consider than money alone.

If you are planning to make a career out of being an author or poet, rather than write one standalone book, it's important to look beyond the surface; beyond whether or not the advance is a good one. Unfortunately, there are often dark forces at work that prevent us from doing so. When most authors are offered a book deal, two little hobgoblins tend to play a starring role in the decisions they make. You will most likely know those hobgoblins by their common names of Vanity and Fear. Fear is a blue-skinned, toothless fellow while Vanity strides around the place in a scarlet silk shirt and perfectly-pressed chinos — never smiling; only smirking, snidely.

Neither of these influencers from the dark side are the kind of company you want to keep while trying to make sound business decisions. This book will hopefully help you resist their lurid charms while making sure your publisher and your agent are fully apprised of everything you want and expect from this agreement.

Twenty years ago, or even ten years ago, the narrative line around publication ran like this: if you are an author plucked from the abyss of obscurity by a gatekeeper in the publishing world, then you should shut-up, nod and agree to whatever they offer. They are, after all, your only route to becoming a Legitimate Author; an author who is known and respected throughout the land.

I'm not totally sure who first made up this legend for the ages. It could very well have been authors themselves. A tale created by the first fledgling commercial writers who were looking to thwart the phantom of imposter syndrome for good by seeking acceptance and validation from noteworthy gatekeepers.

Regardless of who first told the tale, this story has been perpetuated by the traditional publishing industry, and those who profit from it, for decades and, not having much alternative, writers have committed the tale to heart and memory.

The truth is that the modern-day author has numerous options open to them that don't even involve a publishing house. Given that we've now got a choice about how we put our work out into the world, we've also got something we didn't have twenty years ago: bargaining power. Traditional contracts are suitable for very particular people under very specific circumstances. Before you sign on the dotted line, it is prudent to make sure you are one of them.

The Role of **HONESTY**

Remember when I said there was more to a publishing deal than making sure the advance was good? Ensuring the working relationship with your editor is strong and open is probably the first fundamental element of striking a book deal that doesn't directly relate to money. If you choose to create a book with a publisher, you will spend a significant amount of time going back and forth with your editor about changes to the manuscript. Anyone reading this who thinks that their book is perfect and will need no more than the odd comma changing here and there is likely to be in for a bit of surprise once the editorial process starts. The question isn't: 'is your book good as it is?' the question is: 'does your book satisfy readers of this genre on all levels?' A good editor has to ask such questions to make sure they are giving the book the best chances of success, and this will likely mean you'll need to do some revisions.

Because of this, you need to do all you can to make sure that you and your possible new editor are on the same page about what your story is really about. If you are at odds with your editor and your publisher on the above point, the editorial process is likely to be long, laborious and gritty for all concerned. If you self-publish, you'll be able to choose your own editor and choose which revisions you want to make. In the world of traditional publishing, you have to make the relationship work with the editor who is offering you the deal. It requires compassion, kindness, sensitivity and compromise from both sides.

Consequently, determining if a traditional contract is the right choice for you will require a great deal of honesty. If you're honest with your new editor from the get go, it really helps them do their job and understand what the parameters of the relationship are. If you're going to hand over all rights to a piece of work you've toiled over for goodness knows how many months, that's a relatively important thing to establish. If you hold back about the things you really want and the things you really think at the beginning, both you and your editor are likely to find yourself locked into an agreement that doesn't work very well and that neither of you can easily get out of.

Because of this, I wouldn't advise any author to sign a contract before having a conversation with their possible future editor. This might be over the phone or in person, but I recommend a medium that isn't email. You need to get a feel for this person in real time. When you sign a publishing contract, you sign over not just the rights to your work but also a great deal of the income associated with that work. Thus it's prudent to know who you are dealing with and to be honest about who you are and what your primary goal is.

When you're having this meeting, the hobgoblins of Vanity and Fear will pull up a chair to the table. Fear will hiss that you must nod and accept anything that the publisher comes up with. After all, you don't want the publisher to retract the offer. Vanity will whisper sweet nothings in your ear about how wonderful it will be to see your name on a book cover: a badge of acceptance from renowned publishing institutions. Vanity will try to convince you that this is all that matters.

Don't fall for any lines spouted by these untrustworthy rogues.

The publisher made you an offer because they are serious about signing you. The likelihood of them withdrawing because you ask a few questions is small, and frankly, you wouldn't want to be working with a company that demonstrated such fickle behavior from the outset. Besides, you deserve to get more for all the time you've spent creating this book than seeing your name on the cover of it.

So, over the course of the meeting, do all you can do to tune out those two sly hobgoblins and be honest with this potential new colleague about your vision for your creative project. Though it can feel daunting, especially when we're keen not to come across as naïve or high-maintenance, doing so will save you a lot of heartache in the long-term.

DOWN TO
BUSINESS

So. You've asked your agent to organize a meeting or phone call. Or, if you're in direct contract with the person who wants to publish your work, you've organized one yourself.

During the conversation you have with this person, you will need to ask several pertinent questions (I'll outline what all those questions are in subsequent chapters) and ensure you make notes on what answers you are given. After the phone call or meeting, I advise you send an email summarising the key points and giving the editor in question an opportunity to make any amendments to your interpretation of the exchange.

If you have ever worked in an office environment, you probably recognise this process of creating meeting notes and putting them in writing. I'm not suggesting that you do this for every meeting you have with a publishing professional, though you can if you want, but certainly when it comes to the initial chat it's good to ensure it goes on record. Not only does this make anything you've agreed more official, it helps you get in the zone you need to be in to broker the best book deal for you: the business zone.

Yes, for the purposes of this meeting I want you to try and let go of the emotional ties you have to this project and I want you to think of your book as a business asset. I want you to think about the hundreds of hours you've spent writing it, editing and proofing it. I want you to think about the courses you've paid for, the books you've bought, the magazines you've subscribed to, the editors you've hired to get to this point. I want you to think about what writing this book has cost you and everything you've put into it up front, without any solid guarantee of a return on your investment.

Next, I want you to think about the fact that the publisher you're thinking of signing with is going to take away between four to ten times more than you on any book they sell. Slightly more, actually. The average author royalty for ebooks is 25% and the average author royalty for physical copies is 7.5%. And that's on net receipts, not the price the book sells at. So after your advance, you're looking at a small slice of the pie you spent so long baking. The publisher and retailers will get the lion's share.

Why am I asking you to think about all this? Because today you think you only wrote a book because you love writing, or because you wanted someone to read it and tell you they liked it, or because you want to be able to look back one day and say you were published by Penguin or Hachette or HarperCollins. One of these things is likely your main focus today, but our wants shift over time. And when we achieve a huge milestone, like getting traditionally published, our mind often creates all-new milestones for us to reach. And suddenly, you will find yourself wanting to reach more than just the one reader. Or wishing that you make a bit more money from your writing, so you could have more time to write and reach more readers.

There's nothing wrong with this. You should be able to acknowledge your achievement of getting published and maintain the right to be ambitious. But brokering the best possible book deal requires some long-term thinking. Rather than just grabbing what's on the table today, think about how you might feel tomorrow, next week and next year. Think beyond money, what do you want for this piece of work to do, for your readers and for yourself?

The other reason I want you to think about all this is because I want you to recognise the value of your work. The market is fiercely competitive. Very few authors out of the many putting pen to paper are selected for publication by traditional gatekeepers. If someone wants to discuss a book deal with you, then you've got something special in your possession. Something saleable. Something precious. Something someone else wants to pay you for. That puts you in a position of power. If you make an emotional choice based purely on the desire to see your name on the front of a published book, you lose some of that power.

I know this temptation well. I have a confession: me and the hobgoblin named Vanity got jiggy. Not just once, but several times over in my writing career. I lived through this ordeal and survived merely to pass on this harrowing yarn so that you can be stronger than I was. So you might recognise your worth as a creator, and the huge potential worth attached to the rights you are about to sign over.

I'm not suggesting you'll be able to get every last thing you want or that you should use your bargaining power to make unfair demands on the publisher. They have a business to run just as you have bills to pay. But it's certainly worth acknowledging the power you have and leverage it to ensure you get some of the things you really want out of the exchange.

If it helps, imagine each page of your manuscript as a £50 note or the equivalent for wherever in the world you're reading in right now. Treat the exchange ahead as a business discussion where you are in control and you will very likely get a much better level of service from your publisher.

Doing It
BACKWARDS

——

Sometimes, the most valuable things you get out of a book deal are the things that you receive on top of the usual, expected terms such as advances, royalties and exposure. If you are a writer without an agent and a publisher is interested in your work, the first question to ask is if they can recommend some literary agents who might be interested in representing you. If you're serious about being traditionally published, you're going to save yourself a lot of grief if you acquire a literary agent. The rules are a little bit different for poets, but for everyone else, representation is prudent. Even if this time you found a back door into the publishing world through a competition or an open call for submissions or a friend of a friend who once worked at the publishing house, without a literary agent you are going to have to rely on that kind of luck every time you need to seek a publisher.

There are no guarantees that the publisher you sign with today will renew your contract in three years. And then where will you be? Well, I'm not trying to scare monger here and none of us know what the future holds or how a situation will turn out. But there is a strong possibility that without an agent you will wind up back out in the cold, knocking on locked doors and hoping that one of them will open for you again as they did once before. For those who have their heart set on a career in traditional publishing, this is not a desirable outcome and it makes good business sense to protect yourself against this possible scenario.

If an editor wants to publish your work, they should have no problem recommending a few agents to you. If they aren't willing to do this you've really got to question why. Are they going to try and get you to sign a contract that no self-respecting agent would accept? Why would you want to do that when there are so many options for authors with great manuscripts in the post-internet landscape? Make it clear to the publisher you do not want to proceed until you have an agent in place. Put these words in writing and make sure they are clear. If you don't, even if you acquire an agent, there is a chance the editor will tell them you said you were happy to proceed with the terms as is and they won't be able to negotiate anything better.

An agent is much more likely to be interested if you already have an offer — even a verbal one — from a publisher. This is how I acquired my agent. Yes, like everything else in life, I did publishing backward. Most people acquire an agent then get an offer of publication. For me, it was the other way around. This goes to show that despite the kind of advice you'll read in tomes like The Writers' and Artists' Year Book, there are many different routes into publishing and everybody's journey is, to a certain extent, unique.

Regardless of the varied and unique journeys to publication, one thing that seems to hold true for almost every writer I speak to is the value of a good literary agent who is invested in your work. So start your publishing negotiations as you mean to go on: by getting the most career-advancement out of the experience as you can, and make sure you get that added value of an agent into the bargain. Those of you who already have an agent will know why I'm making such a big deal out of this. Don't begrudge your agent their 18%. They will earn it, and much more, over the years by guiding you through an uncertain industry with many pitfalls. Publishers may come and go over you're the years but a good agent will always be there to support you in the next step of your writing career.

A Note About the
SUBMISSIONS PROCESS

——

It's worth mentioning here — before we move on to talking about how to work with publishers — that acquiring an agent does not necessarily guarantee you a publishing deal with any manuscript you write. This is not something many people talk about so before I was traditionally published, I, like most aspiring authors, thought that if I secured an agent then I would never have to worry again about landing a publishing contract. I thought that if an agent represented my manuscript at least one publisher was guaranteed to say 'yes' to it.

Some of the more seasoned writers reading this will be shaking their head in pity at the naivety of 2015 me, and rightly so. You wouldn't be the first person to suspect me of poor judgement, especially given that after two sniffs of white wine I am prone to delivering an unsolicited lecture on all the reasons Grease 2 is better than the original Grease. Hopefully though, the fact that agents aren't necessarily able to secure a publishing contract is news to at least one reader out there, so I don't feel so alone in my naivety.

But seriously, Grease 2 is way better than Grease.

Those wondering why I speak so highly of agents when they're unable to provide any guarantees clearly haven't tried navigating the publishing world solo. Besides anything else agents are, generally speaking, successful at securing publishing contracts for their clients. They often do this by reading the author's drafts and offering suggestions that will make the manuscript more saleable. Once it's ready they will then offer it to editors who they think will say 'yes' to what you've written.

Agents spend a lot of time building relationships with editors and researching market trends to make sure your book is sent to the most likely candidates. They also work with a lot of debut authors whose books won't be released for another year to eighteen months. This gives them an almost prophetic ability to know what the book market will look like in the near future and how your book might fit into it. Even with this insider industry knowledge, there are times when none of the publishers bite.

This doesn't mean the manuscript was bad. For one thing, the agent took your manuscript on because they thought they could sell it to a publisher, so it must have some merit. Agents aren't keen to waste their time. But there are a million other factors that can affect whether your manuscript is picked up or not.

They include but are not limited to: an editor having bought a book just like yours last week (I know we all like to think of ourselves as deeply original, but I hate to tell you there is a lot of evidence for the collective unconscious in the media we produce); the editor may like your book, but is not sure how they can sell it; the editor may have a good sense of the readership their publisher caters to and decide your book won't quite satisfy them for some arbitrary reason.

Although I've thankfully not yet had a manuscript that didn't get picked up, I have had plenty of rejection emails sent to my agent from editors who cite the reasons above for saying 'no' to my manuscript. Some writers get these emails persistently and have to find a way of making peace with the fact that the manuscript they spent so long working on isn't going to find a home in a traditional publishing house at present.

This is understandably a terrible blow to some writers, but it needn't be the end of the world. There are a few different ways to move forward from this. The first is to get straight back on the horse and start writing something new. Even if you already have other manuscripts prepared for your agent to submit, it's good to reconnect with your craft again as soon as possible to remember why you love writing stories and poems so much. It doesn't really have anything to do with big publishing houses. If you complete stories and poems on a regular basis, you likely do so because you derive some pleasure in it. Focus hard on that pleasure. Indulge in it. Over the long-term you will come to understand it as the best bit of the writing business. In a strange way it's much more exhilarating than the temporary high you get when signing a book contract.

The manuscript that was rejected can either go in a drawer for that fateful day when an editor does accept your work and then you can try selling it to them. Alternatively, if you want to get an immediate return on investment for all the hours you put into it, you could independently publish the manuscript and use that for some pin money while you're waiting for your next book to get picked up. Do check that your agent is OK with this, but if they haven't managed to secure you a publishing deal from a traditional house, then they are highly likely to let you look at other means of publication.

Also, don't fall into the trap of thinking that once you self-publish you can never land a traditional contract. I self-published two non-fiction books before I had my first one traditionally published. If anything, an editor at a publishing house will be pleased to work with someone who already has some sense of what it takes to put together a book.

So, to summarise, starting the submissions process with an agent doesn't guarantee you a publishing contract with a traditional publisher, but it does give you your best chance of securing one. If, for any reason, the submission doesn't yield a deal, there are still ways of profiting from the manuscript directly. And, there is always the next manuscript.

WHAT'S IN A
DEAL MEMO?

The next step — before you have that all-important meeting with your future editor — is to request a deal memo. If you have an agent they will request this as a matter of course. If you're working solo for any reason however, it will be down to you. Whatever you do, don't go into a meeting with a publisher without a deal memo. I did this when I first started writing fiction and it wasn't a smart move. Yes, that's embarrassing to admit, but the whole point of this book is to help you to be smarter than I was about this whole process. I made a lot of mistakes I'd like you to avoid and that's not even counting the bottle of £3 vodka I drank at a university party back in 2001.

But I digress.

Don't let the unfamiliar terminology intimidate you. A deal memo is just the official offer in writing from the publisher laying out the key terms. To have any hope of maximising the terms of your contract and ensuring you don't agree to terms that aren't a fit for your expectations, you need to know what the publisher's business proposal is going to be.

In simple terms, a deal memo is a precursor to the contract. A publisher sending a deal memo in no way binds you to accept the contract. It is an offer and nothing more. I don't recommend agreeing to the first deal memo you are offered. It will be full of boiler plate terms that are desirable to the publisher and not necessarily to you. If you have an agent they will need scope to negotiate the terms so refrain from confirming that everything looks fine the way it is either verbally or in writing at this stage.

The next few chapters take you step-by-step through the contents of a standard deal memo. Alongside explaining what you can expect to see, I've also done my utmost to draw your attention to particular elements you need to be mindful of before you agree to go to the next step of signing a contract with a publisher.

You see how I'm looking out for you? Don't mention it. It's like, my calling in life.

THE WORKS &
RIGHTS

—

Even those of us with no legal training can usually decipher this part of a deal memo all by ourselves. The publisher will have listed the work or works they want to buy and what rights they want to buy. They may only want to buy one book from you, but this is less common — at least in fiction. Publishers tend to want to build an author brand, so the likelihood is that you'll be selling them at least two books unless you're writing a one-off non-fiction volume or a poetry collection.

If you're writing in a series, then the deal memo will list the books in the series. If you write standalone books, then the publisher will usually list any subsequent books due as 'Book 2' and so on. By wording the memo this way, publishers are generally understood to be requesting the option on your next full-length work. You will agree a synopsis with your editor before writing the book to ensure it is a fit for the brand the publisher is trying to build for you.

Under rights, you will likely find that the publisher has asked for World English Rights which means they own the rights to publish in English all around the world including America, Australia and New Zealand. Although many authors accept these terms, you might want to think twice before handing over your American rights as either you or your agent could try and sell your work separately to an American publisher.

If you can avoid selling the publisher your translation rights, then it's often more lucrative for you to do so. In the majority of cases, the odds of a publisher getting translation deals in non-English speaking countries for a debut author are not high. You should only sell the rights that the publisher can reasonably prove they can exploit. Although these recommendations come from a general picture of the industry as a whole — and you should be mindful that your book could be the exception — it's usually much better to leave foreign rights with your agent who can pitch them directly to foreign publishers at the Frankfurt Book Fair and the London Book Fair. This is the easiest way of dealing with your translation book rights. If you don't have an agent, you can always look into selling those rights independently.

In addition to stating the language and location of the rights you are signing over, the deal memo will also make it clear how long the copyright term is. Usually this states that the publisher has the rights to publish your work for the full term of copyright (unless at any point the rights revert). In case you don't know, the full length of copyright is your entire life plus seventy years after you die. This might be a point that you want to raise with the publisher as, now that self-publishing is taking off, some people are managing to negotiate more particular terms on this point. But such developments are very much in their infancy so the publisher might be quite surprised by any questions on this score.

This part of the memo will also outline how many words the publisher expects to receive for each book. In my experience if you land within 5,000 words either side of this the publisher won't quibble, especially on a first draft which is subject to quite a few changes. Writing isn't an exact science and most editors are sensitive to the idea that planning your book to a precise word count is a tall order at times.

The proposed delivery date for each book should also be listed. Make sure this is manageable and realistic. I reiterate: a publisher who is worth working with will not want to sign you up to terms that are going to turn your life upside down. This includes unreasonable deadlines.

How many books you will be expected to write per year will vary depending on the kind of books you write. Most people in the commercial fiction world (authors like me who write to a particular genre such as horror, romance or thriller) put out a book every six months. Most literary authors (writers nominated for those wonderful literary prizes who write 'meaningful' stories often about a tortured soul trying to find peace) are expected to write at a slower pace. It takes time to find peace in this world. Due to the number of accolades a book like that can pick up, literary writers can afford to bide their time and slow down their art.

I have written three full-length novels in a year before now alongside a part-time job (which is considered slow by some!), but it wasn't easy and really there is no need to stress yourself out before you've even signed a contract. The thing about launching as a new author is, the less time between books the bigger the splash you'll make. So, if you're contracted for three books, and particularly if you plan to write commercial books, ask if the release date can be pushed back by six months. This way, you can deliver the other two at such a rate that the publisher can release each volume three or four months apart. If you've already written three books and have them sitting on your computer, hurrah! You can agree to the release date stated knowing that you've got a first draft of all the material that's expected of you and the months ahead will purely be about editing and proofing, which admittedly is a big enough job all on its own.

The lesson to take away from the above paragraph is essentially to, yet again, avoid doing what I did. Don't send the first novel you ever write straight off to an agent or publisher. As touched on in earlier chapters, I recommend writing more than one book before you approach a publishing professional. If you do this, you will be able to write on your own timescale and you will always be ahead of the game. If you've already approached publishing professionals and had an offer, now is the moment to buy back as much extra time as you can before the release of your first book, and ask for the delivery dates on the deal memo to be modified as necessary.

Royalties & **ADVANCES**

This is the part where most people learn some unwelcome facts about the financial affairs of traditionally published authors. When they realise their fantasies of swimming around in a Scrooge McDuck inspired-money pool are likely to stay, well, fantasies. At least for the short-term. Long-term, there are big pay-offs for writing traditional books, particularly if you stick to the same genre. But it's important to know that the Scrooge McDuck money pool isn't likely to materialise tomorrow.

There is something of a disconnect between the financial realities of being a traditionally published author and how the world perceives the finances of a traditionally published author. This is because the only time most of us hear about the income of traditionally published authors is when they hit it big, sell a million books in a year, get a six figure advance or become J.K. Rowling. The not-very-newsworthy truth is that these people tend to be the exception rather than the rule.

Very few traditionally published authors are making good money off the back of their books and those that do usually have a long backlist, i.e. it's unlikely but not impossible that you'll 'make your millions' on the back of one book. If you do, congratulations. Time to buy that private jet you've always hankered after. You know, the one complete with its own cinema on board that's programmed to play every Die Hard movie on a loop. Yes, even the terrible fifth one featuring John McClane's son, because why the hell not? You need to celebrate. You have achieved something that very, very few people do.

You deserve that private jet, dammit.

Ahem.

The royalties and advances portion of a deal memo will lay out what monies you are due and when you will receive them. The biggest surprise to most authors is that they don't receive the advance in one big lump sum. The advance is split into instalments. The first instalment is paid when you sign the contract, the second is usually paid when you deliver the manuscript, the third is usually paid when you are published in ebook and the fourth when you are published in paperback. Different publishers are prone to slightly different practices but you will likely see some variation on this theme.

If you bear in mind that your publication day might be six to twelve months away, it does mean you will be waiting some time to get your hands on quite a bit of the money on offer. If more than one publisher is interested in your work, then your agent will be able to conduct an auction. I have been in this situation and it meant I ended up with a higher advance than the one I was first offered. It also meant the deal was more favorable to me on several other levels because the editors involved wanted me to say 'yes' to them and thus knew it was important to offer other perks to signing with them because there was competition for my books.

There is only so much scope for this as it's largely agreed that there are five big publishing houses in the industry — at least in the Western hemisphere — and they have rules prohibiting their editors bidding against each other. So, if it happens that the two editors who want to buy your book work at different imprints in the same company, the bidding can only go as far as the opening offers. If this happens, your focus will likely be not on money — because both parties are offering the same amount — but on other elements such as that imprint's marketing track record and the number of formats you are released in.

When it comes to the percentage you'll take from book sales once you've earnt out your advance, you can expect your royalty rates to look something like this:

Ebook: 25% of net receipts.

Paperback: 7.5% of net receipts.

Hardback: 10% of net receipts.

Audio: 10% of net receipts.

As a debut author, you're very unlikely to see much movement on these numbers. Some digital first imprints offer 50% of net receipts for ebooks and sometimes it's possible to negotiate an increase in royalties after the first 10,000 physical copies are sold. But this is the part of the proceedings you don't need to worry too much about if you have an agent. Your agent will always negotiate the best possible deal they can for you. If you don't have a literary agent, and haven't been able to acquire one, you might want to ask a lawyer who specialises in intellectual property to vet your contract and make some suggestions.

The main reason I'm drawing this part of the deal memo to your attention is so you don't get any nasty surprises when you receive it. I wouldn't want you getting your hopes up for some super-favourable financial terms when the odds are that you're going to see everything I've outlined above.

And that's really just about it. The deal memo is a bare bones summary of the contract laying out all the bits and pieces that agents and authors are most interested in. It's a simple but important document.

Perhaps now that you know what's in a deal memo, you can see why I suggested you get a look at it before you go into the meeting with your editor. You'll want more information on some key elements of this document and on some of the things that aren't mentioned, but it gives you a starting point for discussions.

In summary, after reading the deal memo you should know: what the publisher wants to buy; when they expect the works to be delivered and how long they expect them to be; what formats the publisher want to publish the books in; how much money they'll give you up front; when you'll receive the remainder of your advance and what the royalty rate will be on the books they sell, assuming you earn out your advance. Now that you've got all of this in writing, it's time to do some preparation for your first meeting with an editor.

In the immortal words of Macaulay Culkin: *"This is it, don't get scared now".*

PREPARING FOR AN
EDITORIAL MEETING

By now, you're probably impatient to get into the meeting with your editor, or have the phone call with them, as soon as possible to find out more about this future working relationship. Before that happens, I would recommend doing some of the following preparation.

First of all, complete an internet search for the company online. Take a look at their website, social media and read any news articles about the company's dealings in general. We all want to be treated well in any professional relationship so it's a good idea to get a handle on how this particular company manages theirs. Is their website up-to-date? Does their social media presence show strong support for authors and bookshops? Do any articles cast them in a generally positive light? If there are several articles from authors who have worked with them discussing the terrible experience they had at the hands of this company, then you may want to think twice about working with them. If you don't think twice about it, at least you'll know upfront the price you might pay for the prize of a traditional publishing contract in the worst case scenario.

Once you've looked at the general picture, start to research the writers this publisher works with in your genre. Some writers do this bit of homework without any prompting, but then fall into the trap of looking at only the writers who have hit it big with the publisher's help. They tend to scroll down the list of authors on the publisher's website and say, 'oh, they've published Patricia Cornwell' or Margaret Atwood or Dan Brown and decide, on this basis, that this must be a good publisher to work with. Unfortunately, though it's nice to dream about such a pie in the sky success, it is unlikely that your first book will be a mammoth, record-smashing best-seller, though I wish you all the luck in the world with that.

Consequently, it is more useful to look at how authors are doing at the beginning of their careers with this publisher. Preferably, you will find an author that they've published in your genre in the last three months. Given how many books a traditional publisher puts out per month, this shouldn't be too difficult. Once you've found such a candidate, look at their book rankings and general online presence. After three months are they still ranking high in the top online stores? Is it clear that the author in question had quite a bit of press secured for them? Are their books visible and available? If their books turn up on page three of the Google search or are resting low at the bottom of the Amazon rankings that is not a particularly good sign. Although a lot of writers fixate on getting to the top of the charts right out of the gate, authors who experience this can find their sales spike and then immediately plummet. Though not as 'glamorous' it's actually much better to have solid steady sales over the long-term than a spike in the short term as it means new readers are constantly buying your books and you are consistently building an audience for future works.

If the authors you research are approachable and make themselves available on social media or via email, it is perfectly legitimate to reach out and ask them if they would recommend their publisher. Framing the question positively makes it clear that you are not digging for dirt but looking to establish what kind of experience to expect.

First-time authors often feel shy about reaching out to those with a more established track record, but the truth is most authors are happy to support and advise others in their craft. Most of them remember what it was like when they were just starting out and the consequences of making mistakes they could have avoided if there had been somebody else to guide them. So don't be shy. I'm not going to pretend you'll get a personalised response from Stephen King, he's pretty busy! But if you're approaching someone who is in the early stages of their career or a so-called 'mid-list author', then you are likely to get a response whenever they have time to deliver one.

There's one last bit of research that's worth doing before you go into a meeting with a traditional editor and that's research into book covers and blurbs for books recently released in your genre or those sitting in the top of the charts in online stores. If you go in knowing what kind of covers and storylines are marketable for the sort of story you've written, you'll not only sound more professional, but you will also be able to gauge how knowledgeable your editor is about the genre you're working in and thus the likelihood of them being able to sell a decent number of books for you.

Doing all of this research is no guarantee of signing a better book deal than what you would have otherwise, but it puts you in the best position to. By entering into a publishing contract, you are starting a new business relationship, and consequently, it makes sense to go into the union informed. This way you can make the process from a final draft to publication as smooth as possible for everyone involved.

THE TRADITIONAL AUTHOR MINDSET

Before going into a meeting or phone call with your potential new editor, I recommend getting into what I call the Traditional Author Mindset. This is the name I give to a reasonable outlook adopted by an author who wants to positively engage with professionals in a traditional publishing setting. It largely involves shaking off any resentment you might feel towards the traditional publishing industry. You might be sitting there thinking that you don't harbour any resentment towards the publishing industry, and maybe you are one of the few that don't. Well done for being a better person than the rest of us, your medal will likely be lost in the post but I'm sure the gods are smiling down on you.

Many of us mere mortals do hold some kind of resentment towards traditional gatekeepers when we start out, even if we have to dig quite deep to find it. The resentment often stems from the fact that the system seems arduous and unfair. The writer may have had to endure many rejections and put in a lot of unpaid hours to get to the point of being offered a traditional contract. Others are disappointed with the amount they've been offered in their advance but don't have any other offers so they feel like they have to make do with what's on the table. I have also known authors resent the idea that an editor might have a particular vision for their manuscript, believing they know best on all editorial points for their project.

Dwelling on any of the above thoughts and feelings is not going to make for a fruitful meeting or partnership. It can even lead to authors viewing the publisher as the enemy, rather than a senior partner in their literary success. Although I do suggest thoroughly vetting any legal document you receive from a publisher, treating the people who work for them as the enemy is unhelpful to say the least. Consequently, I believe you should go into the meeting, and all future dealings, in the spirit of sensitive collaboration.

It is unfair, for example, to make demands on your publisher to catapult you to immediate superstardom. They would be as delighted as you if that happened, but the reality is that, for most people, superstardom may never happen and even moderate fame is slowly built in a marketplace that is overcrowded with other authors, books, TV shows and films. Stories are everywhere. A publisher cannot guarantee that everyone will choose to engage with yours straight away.

It is also important to remember that the publisher — and all of its employees — want your book to do well. Putting together a book takes an incredible amount of work: editorial, design, administrative and manufacturing. The publisher does not want all of that work to be for nothing and should do all it can within its budget to help build your profile and the platform for your work. It is in the publisher's best interests for you to succeed, just as it is in yours.

I can't pretend that the publisher is always 'on your side', they will make decisions based on the survival of their company as any company would and on the odd occasion what's good for them might not be good for you, but let's just say that for the most part your interests are aligned.

Remembering all of this will hopefully help you get a handle on any resentment you have towards 'The System'. After all, the person you're about to meet with didn't create the system. They are a cog in the machine, just as you are, and will be doing the best they can to keep the engine whirring.

YOUR EDITOR

—

On the way to the meeting with your editor, or just before you pick up the phone to them, it's prudent to make a list of questions you want to ask about the business of publishing a book with this particular company, and the relationship you'll have going forward. I'm going to make some suggestions based on my experience, but it is my experience and although you and I are both writers, that doesn't mean we are identical personality twins (unless we are, in which case please send me a postcard featuring a guinea pig wearing a wizard's hat).

There might be some things about a deal you really want to know going in that would never feature in my list of priorities. Don't be afraid to ask about it. Going into a creative business relationship is a lot like going into a romantic relationship. You can't be afraid of scaring the other party off. If they're not on the same wavelength as you, it's best you part ways amicably now rather than grow to resent each other after five years of an unhappy marriage.

The meeting is likely to start with the editor telling you how much they like your work. This is always the nice bit for authors. We spend most of our working lives being told by anyone who has a spare minute that our metaphors could be cleverer, our prose could be sharper and our plots could be much neater. So when someone finally turns around to tell us that they like our work, and that person isn't a parent, guardian or the family dog, we almost don't know what to do with ourselves. Often, we are so thrilled somebody 'gets' us and our work that's all we can fixate on.

By all means bask in this golden moment. I can't pretend that there will be hundreds of them to choose from in your writing career so soak it up. Revel. Make hay. Run up the 72 steps of the Philadelphia Museum of Art Rocky Balboa-style. But don't let that good feeling overshadow what you've come to the meeting to discuss, which is the terms of your agreement going forward.

You can get things off to a gentle start by asking about your editor's vision for the book cover. This is a nice creative beginning to the meeting that will also enable you to ascertain right away whether your editor has a good grasp of your genre and how to sell your book. A couple of chapters ago, I suggested you do some research on book covers before going into this meeting. Ideally, you would have visited an online book store and looked at the top ten selling books in your category. This is quite difficult for literary fiction as the covers can differ wildly, but even then there are things you can look at to gauge what kind of package sells well in your arena.

Hopefully when you did this research, you made notes on what kind of colours are used, any common words or themes that pop up in the titles, whether the cover is dominated by text or is more focused on an image. If it's an image, what kinds of images are common in your genre? If you are clear about what the top sellers are doing, then when your editor responds to your question about book covers, you will get an immediate sense of the level of their subject knowledge.

Asking about the vision for the cover is a fair question and a fair method of being sure your editor is up-to-date on the current market. What isn't fair is for you to walk into this meeting with a set idea of how you want your cover to look and insist the editor take your ideas on board. You're not going to like what I have to say next but the truth is — unless you have a background in book cover design — authors are terrible at knowing what should go on the cover of their book. It's not a hard and fast rule. There will be exceptions and sometimes — if you've worked in the industry long enough — you start to get a sense of what kind of elements make for good book covers. Likewise if you do extensive, and I do mean extensive, market research.

But on the whole you're just too close to the project. You want the cover to tell the entire story complete with subplots. You want the models on the cover to look identical to the characters you created on the inside. And even though these sound like fair expectations, you are unlikely to create a strong cover based on these principles. A strong cover embodies one big idea running through the book. It's very difficult for writers, who are so close to the material, to distil a book down in this way. Publishers are often polite enough to ask you if you like the cover they've created, but if you want to work with a publisher, it's important you trust their judgment on matters like the overall sales package.

If your editor tells you they are going to do something wildly different to the designs thrown out by your research, then by all means question it. Ask why they want to go in that direction when all the top sellers in the genre don't follow that pattern. Do they see the book sitting in a different sub-genre than you imagined? If so, get those book covers up on your phone or tablet and take a look through with the editor. Make it a friendly, collaborative discussion. Enjoy the opportunity to get an opinion on how best to sell your book from another publishing professional. There won't be many free opportunities to do that. By the end of this discussion you should have a clear sense of the editor's vision for your book and they should have a clear sense of yours. This is a great starting point for a cooperative and productive relationship, assuming you both like what the other has to say.

For any of you wondering if your book has to look like the others, or asking themselves why you shouldn't encourage your publisher to do something unique and one-of-a-kind, I'm sorry to tell you that most book sales happen because a reader thinks your book is going to be similar to some other books they've enjoyed. Thus, originality with front covers is rarely rewarded. Your story will hopefully have some fresh-feeling twists and turns. When it comes to the cover however, that element needs to be similar enough to others in the genre for readers feel like it's a safe purchase.

Once you've chatted about covers and broken the ice a little bit, you can move onto the questions that are arguably of most importance for authors. Firstly, there's the question of format. What did the deal memo say about formats? Is this book deal an offer for ebook and paperback only? Will the book come out in audio and hardback too? If the book is only coming out in ebook and paperback, make sure that the contract does not state that you are handing over audio and hardback rights. If the publisher isn't going to exploit these you can, and in the world of independent publishing you will make a much greater royalty profit.

If the publisher wants to hang onto rights they are not exploiting, that's a mark in the 'negative' column for this particular deal. At the very worst, rights to formats they are not exploiting should revert to you on paperback publication day. The odds of the publisher exploiting them after that are very slim, so why should they hold onto something that you could be making extra money from? You may not think that it's a big deal, but by only having your books out in paperback and ebook rather than all four formats, you are limiting your readership. Reading habits have changed. Audio is becoming more popular every year and some people want to access your books in more than one medium.

Consequently, I would question why the publisher wants to hang onto the rights they are not exploiting, and I would be very skeptical about signing a contract on those terms... actually, that's not entirely honest. There is no way on earth I would sign a contract under those terms because I've been there and paid the price for it. But it's different for me. I've already been published and I don't want to tell you not to do something if being traditionally published is your big life dream. If that's the case, perhaps you're fine with an ebook-only deal and you don't mind the publisher keeping the rights to the other stuff.

But I just want to flag here that this could wind up being a decision you wish you could reverse. To make sure this deal advances your career as far as possible, you need to reach as many readers as possible. To reach as many readers as possible, you need to be in as many formats as possible. So do think hard before progressing to that contract stage.

The next issue to raise is that of marketing and publicity. Were you surprised that there was no mention of this in the deal memo? It won't be in the long contract either, except in the vaguest of terms. There is no specific stipulation in the contract that says your publisher must complete particular publicity tasks, and even if they tell you what they're planning, there's nothing legally binding to hold them to their promises. Again, this probably changes if you're

Stephen King (though how much publicity does he really need?), but for debut and mid-list authors, you've got little bargaining power when it comes to publicity. It's important to nail down their general strategy as best you can and focus not on extravagant flashy elements such as expensive launches and bookshop tours, but on the things that really sell books.

When you ask your editor about marketing and publicity they are likely to focus on things that most authors like to hear. Things like blog tours and social media posts and maybe even a launch party at a local bookshop. They'll probably talk about creating 'buzz' around your book online. This can all be a lot of fun and it certainly won't harm your book sales. It's wonderful that publishers engage in activity like this and the best part is that it often connects you with book bloggers who are the real unsung heroes of the book publicity world. I'm writing novel six as I finish this book, and there are some bloggers who have been with me since novel one and show continuous loyalty. This kind of interaction connects you with the bigger book community and makes you feel less alone in the publishing landscape.

But when it comes to sales, social media posts and such aren't likely to sell books in the numbers you should be aiming for. Authors like to hear about activity like blog tours because it sounds like there's attention and prestige attached to them, but authors don't always make the soundest business decisions. I'm living proof of this. That kind of activity might open up a few new readers to your name. A few others might take a look at your book cover and add you to their ever-growing to-be-read pile, but in my experience, this is not how you close big sales.

The marketing strategies that make books sell are numerous and change regularly, but if I was signing my first contract with a publisher, I would focus on the following marketing elements. Firstly, a strong pricing strategy. Ideally your publisher will regularly review the price of your book to make sure this element is encouraging sales. Sometimes this will be a price reduction for a limited time, at other times this will be a matter of pricing your book a little higher so that it conveys quality to potential buyers. If your book is out in all formats, you are more likely to be able to sell your ebook at a higher price. This is because an ebook at £2.99 or £3.99 seems a real bargain when compared to a hardback edition at £20.99. Readers feel like they're getting a bargain because they're getting the same content for a much lower price. And you know what? £2.99 is a real bargain for thousands and thousands of your words.

A lot of authors put pressure on their publisher to reduce their ebook to £0.99. They do this because they think that people won't buy ebooks if they are priced higher. They are going for the price cheap, sell big model. I urge you not to put pressure on your editor to reduce the price of your ebook. It's fine to question the pricing model they have in place but they probably will be able to come back with an in-depth explanation as to why the book is priced at that rate. Again, this is an area where you would do well to trust the publisher's sales expertise.

To give you an example of this, I have ebooks on sale with more than one publisher. One publisher is selling my ebooks at a low price hoping that readers will be lured by the promise of a bargain. The other publisher is selling my ebooks at a higher price hoping that readers will be lured by the promise of quality. The ebooks at the higher price are selling a lot better than the ebooks at the reduced price and have done so historically since they were released. This is a reminder that sometimes publishers will make decisions that go against what we intuitively believe to be true e.g. shoppers want bargains. They will go against this idea because they have hard data suggesting that you will profit more if the book is set at a higher price.

The most likely time for an author to pressure a publisher to reduce the price of their book is around publication when we're most hungry for visibility. Again, a good publisher will resist your pleas. They will be thinking about your long-term relationship with these readers and the long-term opportunity to collect pre-orders for all of their authors. Imagine, for the sake of argument, that you pre-ordered an ebook at £2.99 a week before it was published. You loved the look of the cover, and what the book was offering, so you bought it there and then so it would be delivered straight to your tablet on publication day. You also got a warm, fuzzy feeling about the fact you were supporting an author's career by placing that pre-order.

Publication day arrives. Your book is delivered. You read it and, because you're a nice person who likes to support authors, you go to leave a glowing review. When you click through to the book page to do so, you notice that the price has been reduced to £0.99 just two days after publication. You realise this means you were essentially financially penalised for pre-ordering, and for giving a publisher a sense of the demand for this title and for making the author look good for generating sales ahead of publication day. Honestly, if this happened to you would you be likely to pre-order that author again? Or any author for that matter?

Some of you would still pre-order the book but many of you would probably feel like you got ripped off and wouldn't repeat that behavior, which is bad news for the publishing business as a whole. Anything that is bad news for the publishing business is pretty much guaranteed to be bad news for authors.

Why have I taken so much page space to explain this step-by-step? Because it illustrates an important point that authors entering a book contract need to be aware of. We don't like to admit it. We like to think we know what is best for our work at all times, but the truth is sometimes a publisher has more market expertise than you do and bowing to that expertise can be the difference between breaking the market and disappearing into anonymity.

I also want to underline that when you sign a publishing contract, you essentially give up the right to having a final say on your book's price, cover and marketing package. You might have a say, but not the final say. That's the collaborative deal here and it's a pretty fair one. In order to make your book the biggest success possible, a publisher needs to have control of all these elements, otherwise they can't exploit them to the full extent they need to. If you're uncomfortable with the fact that you might not get a say in your cover or that you won't have control over your book's marketing strategy, then you need to think very carefully before signing a traditional deal.

Those with an entrepreneurial spirit might be better suited to

independently publishing the book where all of the control (and all of the expense and all of the problem-solving) is the domain of the author. In your initial meeting with an editor, it is probably inappropriate to ask about the pricing of your ebook as this might be something discussed over several team meetings, but it should be perfectly fine to ask what kind of pricing strategies they tend to favour and why.

What else sells books besides a solid pricing strategy? Mailing lists work well. Ask your publisher if they have a mailing list and how they use it. Ask if your book is likely to make it into one of their newsletters. Whatever their response, and however you decide to publish, you would be wise to start your own newsletter now. Offer readers a free short story or poem to sign-up and start building relationships with the customers you're going to be serving. What do they enjoy in a book? What don't they enjoy? What books have they already read in your genre? What's on their to-be-read pile? What formats do they like to read in? Knowing all this will give you the best chance of serving their reading needs. If you're looking to sell a book, either traditionally or through the indie route, that's need-to-know information.

Other than newsletters, which is really likely to be a joint effort between you and the publisher, you should expect to hear about some online deals they want to sell you into. Bookbub is currently considered the king of all online promotions, and I have heard of some authors offering to swap their last piece of enchanted Turkish delight to get featured in a Bookbub deal. It's important to underline for legal reasons that was a joke, and Bookbub is in no way involved in the trade of black market enchanted Turkish delight or any other kind of enchanted confectionery.

Alongside Bookbub, there are also promotions like Kindle Monthly Deals and Kindle Daily Deals. You need to be aware of the fact that your publisher has no guaranteed way of getting you into these deals. They will, at this point, likely be experts at pitching to these companies, but you won't be the only author they are pitching. Even if you were the people selecting books for these promotions might choose to go another way. Although your publisher can't guarantee your place in such deals, and it is deeply unfair to hold it against them if they don't have any luck, you do want to know that they are at least putting your name in the pot. With this in mind it is definitely worth establishing this in the meeting.

By now you might be wondering what your publisher actually can guarantee in terms of marketing strategies and making bulk sales. Assuming that the publisher has got the cover, the title, the blurb and the pricing right, the best use of advertising money outside deals run by major websites is targeted online advertisements. These are usually run through Amazon and Facebook, though other websites are available, and enable the vendor to target readers of the genre within different age groups and territories.

This is the most likely method of selling books on a large scale, unless you are personally willing to do a huge amount of content marketing, so ask your editor where they tend to place targeted advertisements and how long around publication they run those advertisements for. A month around publication day is reasonable. If they're running a promotion — e.g. a £0.99 deal — they will need to run advertising to promote the deal, otherwise how will people know about it? So check that your publisher is prepared to spend money on targeted advertising for the book both at full price and when it's having a price reduction.

If you've written a literary novel — i.e. a novel that doesn't fit into a straight genre like horror, romance or science-fiction — ask what awards the publisher is thinking of putting you forward for. If this seems like a presumptuous question, you should know that this is the primary method by which literary works gain visibility. So don't be shy about it. If you're a literary author sitting in a meeting with an editor from a traditional publishing company, this is a legitimate question.

Getting reviews in places like national newspapers and well-known literary magazines will also help your book sales. Those of us who write genre fiction tend not to show up in these places because of the general snobbery around genre fiction, but we probably need it less than you. When I write historical romance I know there are already readers out there actively looking for their next book set in Medieval England. You however, have to convince readers that your coming of age classic about a factory worker living in 1970s Croydon is the book they should read next. It helps to have the critics on your side for a job like that.

Whilst we're on the subject of reviews, regardless of the genre you write in, ask your editor how they ensure a new book receives reviews on publication. Reviews are the life blood of an author's career. They provide social proof to readers that some people have read — and hopefully enjoyed — your work, encouraging them to give it a go for themselves. Your publisher might use platforms like Netgalley or Amazon Vine; they might engage book bloggers or specialist magazines. Whatever their approach, it's important to confirm that they have a range of strategies in place to garner these all-important reviews. You may be asked for a list of people they can send an advanced review copy (ARC) to. Try and name a few people who you've connected with on social media if you can. But don't worry if your list is short. Although I recommend doing all you can to help your publisher where you can, collecting reviews is ultimately their responsibility.

The last thing that it is prudent to discuss with a possible editor is the direction of the stories if you're writing in a series. On the whole, publishers like series. A series is more likely to give them a solid return on investment than standalone books because, by their nature, they encourage readers to buy more than one volume by that author. But you still need to check in with your editor about the direction you see the books going. If you plan to end your space opera on a note of sublime tragedy and your editor is insistent that the books need to have a happy ever after, there is probably some negotiating to be done.

Ensure that you and your editor also see eye-to-eye on the books tonally. Are you trying to write something that is poker-straight serious? Does your editor think the whole story would be better off played for laughs? That's the kind of thing you should find out at the start.

To be clear, I'm not suggesting that you should stick doggedly to your ideas about what the book should look like, nor am I suggesting that you should take offence to your editor's ideas or silence them. If you want to work with a traditional publishing house, that kind of attitude isn't going to be the best way forward. Remember what I said before about the need for compassion, sensitivity and compromise? It runs both ways. You would like the editor to be sensitive to your vision and they, by the same token, are trying to do their job to the best of their ability, so it's important to be sensitive to their suggestions and give them the hearing out and discussion they deserve.

If you like the answers to all of the above questions then there's a good chance you and your editor are going to work well together and that it is worth progressing to the next phase of the contract. If some of the answers you get leave you a little bit uncertain then you might want to go with another offer if you have more than one editor interested, or do some research into the indie author route. There are more details later in this book about whether an independent publishing route or a traditional publishing route will work best for you, but at least be assured that if you want to get your work out there you have some options on how you do that and you are perfectly within your rights to explore all of them.

PART 2:

WHEN

The Publishing
CONTRACT

———

Once you've had your meeting with the editor or editors interested in your manuscript, you will be expected to say whether or not you'd like to accept the offer from the publisher. Once you've accepted an offer, the publisher will create and issue a contract. Though the deal will not be sealed until the contract has been signed and returned to the publisher, it's quite rare for authors to back out once they've said yes to an offer.

In fairness, after discussions with your editor and your agent or lawyer, there should be few, if any, surprises in the long form contract. There are, however, still a couple of areas that you will want to pay particular attention to and perhaps ask your agent or lawyer about before saying 'yes' to an offer or agreeing to sign the contract.

The first is the option clause. You haven't even delivered the finished version of the first manuscript yet, but publishers will use the contract as a place to call dibs on the next thing that you write. When I first started out in publishing, I was signing contracts that said the publisher had the option to offer me a deal on my next full-length work. It didn't state if it was fiction or non-fiction. In fact no stipulations about it were made in any detail.

At first I was cool with this. I had my hands full just trying to write the books I was contracted for because, as we've established, I didn't go about traditional publishing the smart way and had a full plate from the get go.

But then, after a while, a funny thing happened. It was like something in my mind burst open and all these ideas came flooding out about future books I could write. Not all of them were ideas I would follow to conclusion, but I wanted the option of selling them to the best possible publisher for the genre or the option to independently publish them myself. So I asked my agent to alter the option clause to state that the publisher was entitled to read and offer on the next full-length work in that series. That meant if I wrote an epic romance novel at any point, I had some options about what I did with it and who I offered it to. If you're not writing in a series, then it would be polite to offer the next full-length work in the same genre. This, I think, is a fair compromise. The publisher has first refusal on the next book in the genre they're trying to build your profile in, but if something different and extraordinary comes out of the pen in the time you're contracted, you are within your rights to find the most lucrative method of putting it out into the world.

It also meant that I wasn't condemned to write in the same genre for all eternity. As long as I met the deadlines for my contract, I could write other works in any genre I chose, whenever I chose. In short, your boilerplate option clause is quite limiting to your career. It packs you up in one box and tends to trap you there. Asking for slight tweaks to this clause can give you a lot more freedom to write different kinds of stories, perhaps under different pen names, and having the freedom to sell each one to the highest bidder.

Alongside the option clause, I recommend taking a close look at the reversion clause. This is essentially an explanation of when and how the rights revert back to the author. Traditionally, rights reverted if the book went out of print, but obviously with the dawn of ebooks that became a complicated definition. Consequently, many publishers now state a minimum amount that they have to earn for you in royalties to hold onto the rights. Make sure the amount is reasonable. My very first contract was very much in the publisher's favour in this respect. You can avoid this by querying the terms of reversion and discussing with your agent any reasonable changes to what the publisher has proposed.

If you do get the rights back to the books, you can repackage them and independently publish them at a higher royalty rate, giving you the chance to reinvigorate the income from that particular asset. The financial realities of being an author mean it is prudent to exploit any and all opportunities for staying fiscally afloat. So don't be a smart upstart like I was. Be wise. Be solvent.

THE REALITIES OF
TRADITIONAL PUBLISHING

So you've done all your research. You've met with your editor, you've asked them all the important questions and you've checked in with your agent about the option and reversion clauses. You've asked yourself: what would Buffy Summers do? And now you're starting to weigh up if it's right to accept the offer and sign on the dotted line.

I think that hearing a little more about the realities of being a traditionally published and an independently published author will help you make that decision. Given the focus of this book, it seems fitting to first address the general experience of traditionally published authors.

When it comes to finances, there may be a few surprises for those of you who think a traditional publishing contract is a lucrative model for making money. It can be, but you often have to wait much longer than expected for the pay-off because traditional publishing moves slower in almost all respects when compared to indie publishing. This is in part due to the large number of books each company, and by proxy each editor, is managing. The figures are, at times, eye-watering!

Most traditional publishers in the UK pay their authors twice a year and those payments are often paid three months in arrears. To break it down, royalties are usually paid at the end of March and the end of September. The March payment consists of all the royalties earnt from your books between July and December of the previous year. The September payment consists of all the royalties earnt from your books between January and June of the same year.

To give you a workable example from my own experience, one of my books came out on the 1st of July 2019. All of the royalties accrued from books sold between the 1st of July 2019 and the 31st of December 2019 were due at the end of March 2020 — of course, you only receive a payment if you earn out your advance. Any royalties accrued from books sold between 1st of January 2020 and 30th of June 2020 would be paid in September 2020 — again assuming you've earnt out any advance. So you see, although you might have a book released in July, you wouldn't receive any royalty payment for it for another nine months, and that is only if you have sold enough copies to earn out the advance.

That said, remember the terms of your deal memo. You do receive an advance instalment on publication day so, depending on the size of the advance, you will still receive some money before that first royalties statement, whether you earn out or not. It's wise to note that any amount due after the advance payments have been made might be a long time coming.

In the spirit of full disclosure, there are other factors that can delay payment of any monies due to you. If your book is sold in physical format such as hardback and paperback, your publisher will hold back some of the royalties as protection against any books that might be returned and you often won't see those monies for a year after the book is sold. The percentage retained to protect against returns will vary from publisher to publisher and from format to format, but it generally ranges between 10% and 20%. Depending on your sales, this can amount to a substantial sum of money and the terms of the contract will be clear about the fact that you will experience a delay of around a year before you receive it.

In the chapter on the traditional author mindset, I explained that sometimes your publisher has to make decisions that are good for them and not for you in order to make sure their business remains operational. This is one of these instances, but if you take the long-term view, it is not good for you if a publisher you've signed a contract with goes bankrupt. So, in a roundabout way, though it may not feel it when you get the first glimpse of your royalties statement, this is also good for you and indeed all authors published through that publishing house. Just don't go buying a 1961 Ferrari GT until you see what your royalties statement looks like. I know you want to cruise around with your friends and pretend you're in a cut scene from *Ferris Bueller's Day Off*, we all do. But sometimes — even though Ferris wouldn't agree — we have to be pragmatic.

It's also worth noting here that not all publishers adhere to the March/September payments model. Some digital first and digital only imprints do pay their authors monthly (albeit often three months in arrears). If you sign-up to this kind of imprint, questioning what happens to the rights of the non-ebook formats e.g. paperback, hardback and audio is prudent. No publisher, regardless of their model, should be hanging onto rights they can't or won't exploit when you have the option to exploit them yourself and make more money. Some digital first/digital only imprints do really well; some do really well with certain authors and not others. If you write in romance be particularly careful about signing your ebook rights away as according to early-2020 data from K-lytics, almost 80% of romance books sold on Amazon are in the ebook format. That's potentially a lot of money you are signing away if the terms are not favourable.

Your editor will likely give you periodic updates on your sales figures, but those figures won't help you understand how much the twice-yearly payments will be because you don't know what price the publisher has sold each individual unit for until you receive your royalties statement. This means, as a traditionally published author, you will be largely in the dark about your earnings for most of the year. Your royalties statement may therefore end up being a pleasant surprise or a nasty shock, and unfortunately, there is no way of telling which until you have the statement in your hand. The good news is that alongside royalties statements, twice a year you will receive other income such as your advance payments and, if you register with the British Library for Public Lending Right payments, you can also receive payments when readers check your books out of libraries.

Hopefully from this summary you can see that income from traditional book contracts is not a very certain business and should not be singularly relied upon to pay your essential bills until you've generated a back list of books which will likely earn you a solid minimum payment. Even then, it is probable you will need to supplement your book royalties with other streams of income. In general, it is unwise to be beholden to one employer or provider when it comes to your finances anyway, as many of us have sadly come to understand the hard way during the recent pandemic.

Some of you may be looking at this and thinking 'my God, are there ANY perks to being traditionally published?' Of course there are! The last thing I would want any reader to take away from this book is that there are no upsides to being traditionally published. That would be very unfair to the industry. Remember that this is the portion of the book where I want to level with you about some hard realities of the journey. Some of you might not give a fig that you only receive financial updates twice a year. And all power to you! We all have different priorities. But for anyone for whom finances are a priority, it's good to know up front that this particular element of traditional publishing is more complicated than it might at first seem.

One of the things a lot of traditionally published authors enjoy about having the backing of an established publisher is that they don't have to worry about formatting their book, designing their book, buying ISBN numbers, or selling it into bookshops. All of that should be taken care of by the publisher and the bulk of the marketing and promotion should be too. I can't promise you won't have to do any marketing if you sign with a traditional publisher. The sad truth is that you will probably have to do more than you might expect, but at the very least they should be ensuring that your book gets some reviews with interfaces like Netgalley. They should be sending copies of your books out to magazines and newspapers that are likely to read them, and they should organize a handful of events in small bookshops, libraries or other appropriate venues. They should also, as previously mentioned, be running targeted advertising, so although you might be asked to set-up a blog or build a social media presence, these other elements should be taken care of. If they are not being taken care of, or you see any signs in your initial meeting that these elements aren't a priority, you should ask your agent to raise it with them.

Alongside the publisher handling the logistical elements of manufacturing and promoting the book, you will also have at your disposal a full editorial service which should include a developmental edit to let you know which parts of the story are working and which need revision, a copy edit to make sure the grammar is correct and consistent throughout the manuscript and a proofreader to catch any final mistakes. You will also get the opportunity to proof the document and make any necessary adjustments before it goes to press. Editorial feedback for revisions is one of the biggest costs for independent publishers and they have to find a way of paying for this all by themselves. When you sign a traditional contract the publisher will take a large proportion of the royalties, but they should be providing all of the services previously listed in return.

For authors who simply want to write and don't want to be involved in the business aspects of publishing, the traditional route is an attractive option. One issue to be aware of is that although an editor will be assigned to you in the beginning — likely the commissioning editor who agreed to buy your manuscript — there is quite a high staff turnover among the big publishers in the industry. As a result, you may find the person who bought and championed your work leaves the company and you are assigned a new editor who may not be as enthusiastic about your books or perhaps doesn't see eye-to-eye with you on the direction the stories should take. This can happen more than once with the same publisher.

I have had my fiction published by two major houses, and at each company I have worked with three different editors. I will possibly work with a few more before my current contract is completed. This can be a disconcerting element of traditional publishing for the author. Certainly the first time it happened to me I was very unsettled by it. It's sometimes difficult to move on when you build a relationship with an editor who enjoys your work and then have that relationship end abruptly. It's kind of like the feeling we all got when *Firefly* was cancelled; that stark realisation that real closure is no longer within our reach.

As that new editor commissions new books that are more to his or her tastes, you can also find that promoting and marketing your work becomes less of a priority. Especially if the sales figures are not as healthy as the publisher had hoped. Given all the effort that goes into writing a book, it can be heartbreaking to see your work being pushed aside in favour of books from other authors. But I have to stress that this is a worst case scenario. If you work with a smaller publishing house, staff turnover will still happen but it will likely be a little less frequent. The editors at the larger houses are also often keen to help authors through any transitional period, even if it's a bit rocky at times.

Another reality to bear in mind when it comes to signing a traditional contract is that you are signing away control. In my experience, the decision to sign with a traditional publisher or explore independent publishing largely depends on this point: how much control you like to have over your creative projects. As previously mentioned, you will not have the final say on the cover, the price, the marketing or any other part of the package except what is inside, and even then you will be expected to make revisions based on your editor's comments. Some authors really struggle with letting somebody else into the creative process and handing over these elements to the publisher, so think carefully about your personal feelings in this regard before you sign the contract. Once the contract is signed, getting your rights back is usually expensive and complicated.

As signalled by my description of royalties statements, you will not have immediate access to information about your title as a traditionally published author. Editors are managing hundreds of different titles across the year and, quite reasonably, do not have time to update all authors on a daily basis about sales, marketing and profits. At best you will get updates on some of these things every few months. If you are busy getting on with your next book, then you might not notice that a couple of months has passed since you last spoke to your editor. Some writers however, become frustrated by the lack of communication and don't respond well to not knowing what is happening with their product. Authors in this boat find the wait between sales updates excruciating. If you are uncomfortable with this level of uncertainty, again, please think carefully before saying yes to the traditional route.

Perhaps the last important reality to understand about traditional publishing is that when you sign the contract, your rights to the books specified are locked into that contract. This means you don't have any flexibility to manipulate that material in other ways that might help you raise your profile. Examples of this include giving the first book in a series away for free to simulate interest in reading the rest of the saga. In short, signing a contract does limit what kind of supporting marketing activity you can do as an individual. If your publisher has kept their marketing promises, then this shouldn't be too much of a problem. If however the publisher does not market your book as agreed, there will be limited options for you to make up the difference.

The Realities of
INDEPENDENT PUBLISHING

In many respects the realities of independent publishing are the reverse of those explored in the traditional route but, to be clear about exactly what this means, let's go through each point one at a time to ensure you have sufficient detail. As with traditional publishing, I'm going to start with the financial implications of the independent publishing route.

In the last chapter, there was some discussion about the fact that publishing through the traditional route can often be quite slow. In the independent arena however, the author sets the publication schedule. This might mean that you decide you only want to write a book once every three years, but if you're keen to get as much of your work out there as quickly as possible, it also gives you the opportunity to embrace the rapid release model where you put out a book every month or two. It's worth noting that most authors who use this model write a stack of books before they release their first so that they're always ahead. Nobody wants to think that they can't take time off if they're sick or need a holiday, so whichever route you choose through publishing, make sure it promotes good psychological and physical health.

In addition to being able to put your book out sooner rather than later, as an independent publisher you will also receive payment sooner rather than later on most independent publishing platforms. In some cases you can receive payment for your work within 24-hours. This is a relatively new innovation and can be achieved through the Payhip website, which I first heard about through Joanna Penn who runs *The Creative Penn* website (a must-visit for anyone even contemplating independent publishing). Payhip represents the latest wave in indie publishing, which is to bypass online stores like Amazon and sell your work directly to readers. This said, payment structures like Payhip are still in development. On the whole when using other platforms, you receive your royalties statement at the end of each month and these payments are transferred directly into a nominated bank account.

Even receiving payments monthly however is a lot swifter than the payments received in traditional publishing. This enables you to get a more up-to-date picture of your finances. The fact that you can track your finances in real time also helps you to track the success, or otherwise, of other elements of your business. For example, if you try out a new marketing strategy and your finances improve directly afterwards, you know that marketing strategy was likely to have contributed to that success.

In the traditional publishing arena it is pretty much impossible for an author to know whether any of their activity is having a direct impact on sales. There are ways of checking where you are ranking on websites like Amazon and Kobo, but because of the way the algorithm works, a rise in rank doesn't necessarily mean you are selling more books so it's difficult to track.

Consequently, an author who is traditionally published will not be able to easily ascertain whether posting to their Facebook page or sending out a newsletter to their mailing list is effective as a marketing strategy. At least not in a timely manner. The sales figures from this month will be at least three months away.

Some writers argue against the independent publishing route stating that sales are much less likely. I always I hate to be the one to break it to those people that traditional publishing hardly guarantees sales either. The main difference is that the responsibility for these sales is not something an independent author can just offload on to someone else, it rests with them. Understandably, some writers are deeply uncomfortable with being responsible for their own sales and prefer to shift that responsibility to the publisher so that they can focus solely on the craft of writing. For some writers, independent publishing is too akin to a job in sales and is simply not a fit for the skills they have.

Other writers relish the opportunity to be in control of their own business strategy and to know week-by-week, month-on-month how the books are performing in the market so they can make any necessary adjustments to their strategies and sell more books. Hopefully as you are reading this section of the book, you are already starting to think about which camp you most naturally fall into. As I touched on earlier, twenty years ago this choice wasn't really available to authors, but now that it is, it's worth taking some time to think about which of these two perfectly valid publishing routes would be the best fit for your personality.

A further financial reality to consider when it comes to independent publishing is that it is not possible to publish quality books for free. Occasionally I cross paths with people who want to discredit this claim. They tell me that they do all of their marketing, their editorial work, their administrative work, and their production work themselves and thus, for them, independent publishing is free. Although they are correct in the fact that they haven't paid anything out in terms of hard, cold cash, they have paid with something else: their time. All of the time spent doing the administrative, editorial and production-based tasks was not spent writing — i.e. creating new assets to entertain and inform readers.

In this respect, there is another cost to the independent publisher who believes they are publishing for free by doing everything themselves. If they are not spending their time creating new assets, they are slowing the rate at which their business can grow. Moreover, time is the one thing in this world that we can't create more of. Therefore, there may be a personal cost to people who choose to independently publish in this way. We can always make more money but we can't make more time. I know. This is a deep thought. I found it on Pinterest.

The takeaway from all this is that, as an independent publisher, you will pay to produce your books either with money or precious time. Publishing a book to a professional standard and marketing it accordingly will cost you one way or another. This means independent publishing requires a certain level of investment up front from the author.

Over my time in independent publishing, I have seen the conversation around money and investment shift quite considerably. Ten years ago most authors were talking about how amazing it was that you could publish your book for free by using print on demand services. In most cases these authors didn't spend any money on cover design, they often bypassed editors and proofreaders, they often didn't get their books professionally typeset and some of them didn't even pay for an ISBN number.

It stands to reason that if you bypass these elements when creating a book you can do it very cheaply indeed, perhaps for free. But there is a far greater cost to the quality of the product that you are putting your name on and that customers are buying in good faith, believing this is money well-spent. People who bought independently published books during the dawn of the Kindle revolution will likely have been disappointed by much of what they found. Independent publishing had yet to develop into the rich and vibrant industry it is today, so the quality of most products was quite low.

Somewhere in the last five years or so , there has been a shift in how people produce published books and their attitude towards this process. The focus has become publishing to a traditional standard even if it costs money and instead of talking about how cheaply they can produce a book, people now talk about their book earning out. But whereas a traditional publisher is trying to ensure the author earns out their advance, an independent author is trying to ensure the book earns out the amount they spent to produce it.

As an independent publisher, if you wish to create a product of quality and integrity, you can expect to pay for the following services: a developmental editor, a copy editor, a proofreader, a cover designer or cover design software, an ISBN number for all formats, a possible fee for uploading your book to self-publishing platforms like Ingram Spark and any promotional costs associated with the marketing and publicity of your book. Not to mention the time you spend doing all this when you could be writing another book to make more money.

On the surface most people don't think there's much of an incentive to sign a traditional contract if they can keep full control of their project and make higher royalties by independently publishing (depending on format and platform you're generally looking at between 35% and 85% of royalties compared to 7.5% and 25% of the traditional model), but it should not be underestimated how quickly and easily an independently published project can take over your life when you are working alone with little backing. Careful consideration should be given to the time it requires, especially if you have a family who you are responsible for or would suffer if you spent less time with them. Being an independent publisher means effectively starting your own business and that not only places huge demands on you, but can require significant sacrifices in the lifestyle you have become accustomed to that affect those you love.

It's not all doom and gloom when it comes to the topic of independent book production however. Once you find an editorial team that you enjoy working with and you hire on a contract basis, the odds are you will be able to stick with those people for a significant portion of your publishing career. Remember how I said some publishers have high staff turnover? If you assemble a team full of freelancers who enjoy working with you, then the odds are you will be working with them for some time. This introduces some stability into what can be a very uncertain process and makes it feel less lonely.

Self-publishing is really a misnomer and that is why I have largely referred to it as independent publishing in this book. The odds are that you will not be doing everything by yourself if you publish a book independently. You will need a team to support you even if you're some Super Bad Ass Book Ninja (yes, they are a thing, why do you ask?) who understands how to edit, design, market and produce. There are only so many hours in a day and you will need support at some point.

The other positive a lot of people are drawn to when it comes to independent publishing is the amount of control involved. With a traditional publisher you might get a say in the blurb and the price, but it's unlikely that you'll get the final say. In the independent publishing world however every decision is down to you. The great thing about that is you can make constant adjustments to ensure your business is running in as streamline a fashion as it possibly can. The downside is that every decision is your responsibility, and sometimes if you've tried a lot of different things to make a book work and it still isn't selling, it doesn't feel as though there are really many places to turn to for support. A publisher however, has whole teams dedicated to the selling of books and when you sign a contract with them — although you sign away your control — you also sign away the responsibility.

It's not that there are no support groups in the indie community. There are many collectives on Goodreads, Facebook and The Alliance of Independent Authors that has a network of writers all supporting each other to get the best possible results. But there are no guarantees that a project will work and if it doesn't, it is your money and your time that has been sacrificed for the experiment. When you think about it in these terms it becomes more understandable that publishers are so careful about how much money they offer in their advances and how many royalty payments they make to authors per year. Lots of books succeed but a whole lot of other books fail, and if yours is one of them that could come at a great cost to you if you're an independent publisher.

Whilst I'm still on the realities of independent publishing, I think it's worthwhile dispelling a few myths. The most frequent myth I hear regurgitated is that independent publishing is the same as vanity publishing. For those of you who are unfamiliar with vanity publishing, it usually refers to a system where a company asks you to pay them to publish your book. The irony of this is that you are much more likely to hear the swish of Vanity's silk shirt in traditional publishing than in the independent publishing community.

I say this as someone who has succumbed to Vanity; succumbed to the writer's fantasy of having a publisher tell you how amazing your work is and seeing my name on the front of a hardback book in Waterstones. I can't deny to you that I felt good in that moment, but the truth is that if I wasn't so hot for the acceptance of a publisher, I could have achieved that same goal as an independent publisher because of programs like Ingram Spark. Independent authors can now distribute to bookshops, including national bookshops, for very little cost and I would have been making greater royalties on that book if I'd gone for the independent route. I don't regret it because it felt good and I really enjoy the collaborative nature of working with publishers, but now that I've experienced it and know there are other options out there, I may make different choices in the future depending on the nature of the creative project I'm working on.

The other myth that is perpetuated about independent publishing is that once you have chosen that route you cannot ever hope to be picked up by a traditional publisher. I am always quite surprised to hear this because that's exactly what happened to me. To prove that you can do both, I self-published this book even though I'm currently contracted by a traditional publisher to write fun murder mysteries featuring a crime-solving librarian.

Look at me, Mum, no hands!

This myth is linked to one of the most difficult realities independent publishers have to face which is the snobbery of some traditionally published authors towards us. Thankfully, for the most part, this attitude has mostly died out but there are still some authors who are insecure about these entrepreneurial trail blazers, who are not only publishing books on a more regular basis than them, but making a decent amount of money doing it. Consequently, some of them would like you to believe that traditional avenues are closed to you.

My favourite example of this snobbery from my own experience was during a meal I shared with some traditionally published authors before a Q&A

event. I was also traditionally published by that point, but, without asking about other people's experience around the table, one of the authors in question started to talk about a woman she knew who had independently published her book. She said this woman had exclaimed on her publication day: "I'm so proud of myself! I'm a published author!" and this author admitted to privately thinking: "No, you're not. It's not the same." She talked about this at length before finally turning to me and asking: "So how did you get into writing?"

Thus far I had been doing a pretty stellar job of forking battered fish into my mouth so I could keep quiet whilst listening to this somewhat self-entitled rant. Should your dietary choices and requirements allow for it, I can recommend this as a strategy for self-restraint. It's certainly more pleasurable than biting your tongue. At that juncture however, I really had little choice but to reply: "actually, I started out as a self-published author and then got picked up by HarperCollins."

The author's face drained of colour. Not because she found herself sitting at a table with a self-published author, but because she was embarrassed to have spoken the way she did in front of someone who had used that route as a way of impressing a traditional publisher. She did what she could to recover herself and truly I did not say what I said to embarrass her. It was just the honest answer to the question she had asked. That said, I'll admit to hoping that having met me she reassessed her attitude towards other independent publishers or, at the very least, was a little more careful about how she expressed her opinions in future.

It is highly likely that if you choose the self-publishing route you will come into contact with people who think you are doing it because you couldn't get a publisher. They will also assume your work is inferior to those books that have been traditionally published when in truth, assuming you invest in the process, the opposite is more likely to be true. A traditional publisher, after all, is trying to publish tens of books every week and you are only trying to publish one book at a time. Therefore, it is logical to assume that you will put more focus, energy and effort into that one book than a publisher can with many books over the course of a week or a month. Due to the fact that we have lived so long with the traditional model, people don't think about independent publishing in these terms, but the difference in quality between traditionally published and independently published books is narrowing and in some cases, independently published books have been produced to a higher quality and with more creativity.

In order to achieve this, the independently published author often needs to pass parts of processes onto other people via paid online services, subscription-based author platforms, the editorial team you select and perhaps a digital assistant. But for most people those support mechanisms are decided luxuries when they're first starting out. Unless you have a lump sum to invest up front, they can often only be attained once a lot of hard work has already been put in solo and you are making a decent amount of money from book sales to justify hiring team members and investment in platforms and services.

You'd be forgiven for thinking that I was attempting to turn you off independent publishing by revealing the somewhat complicated truth about life in that particular arena but this is not the case. I relish the opportunity to create something independently, but I don't think it's fair to let people enter into this kind of project without appraising them of the realities. There are of course many positives to independent publishing, and in 2020 it is possible to do almost everything that a traditional publisher can do, including: putting your book out in all formats; getting your book into bookshops; translating your books into different languages; having your book narrated in audio format; entering your book for awards and prizes, and be part of collective organisations that serve authors and help them network.

Consequently, if you are one of those people that prefer to be in control wherever possible, you might find a traditional contract stifling and restrictive. If you choose this route you must be aware of the fact that you are sacrificing writing time to create a product, but if you relish that creative opportunity to call all the creative and commercial shots, then you might find yourself more at ease with the independent publishing route.

DECISION TIME: MAJOR FACTORS

Now that you've had time to digest all of the information in this volume so far, it's time to make some decisions about your career in the world of publishing. Are you a writer who would much rather just focus on the craft of writing? Are you happy to to sign over control of the sales package to your publisher? Are you a person who works better as part of a collaborative effort? Are you naturally compassionate, sensitive and open to taking constructive feedback? Are you OK with only receiving financial updates a couple of times a year? If this sounds like your preferred method of working, then traditional publishing might be the best fit for you.

Although the realities I stated earlier about traditional publishing still stand, if you choose this route you will have the relief of knowing that once you've sent in your final corrections on the manuscript, you don't have to spend hours designing a book cover, formatting a manuscript, uploading it to all retail platforms, writing your own blurb, ensuring you have the correct key words in place to ensure visibility on online bookstores or arrange targeted advertising on numerous websites. Remember, if you don't do all this yourself as an independent publisher you will need to pay others to do it for you, so you pay for all the extras a publisher takes care of in either time or hard cash.

After all I've shared with you, you may instead be considering the independent route. Are you are a person who doesn't like other people having the final say in your creative projects? Does the idea of having to make changes to your manuscript that you might not agree with concern you? Do you find the idea of only getting an update on the financial picture twice a year anxiety-inducing or frustrating? Do you have an entrepreneurial spirit? Are you able to effectively delegate the parts of the business you're not as savvy about to other people? Are you willing to invest additional time and money, alongside writing time, to develop your literary profile? If you've answered yes to most of these questions then I would think hard and long about entering into a traditional contract. It sounds as though you might find some aspects of the traditional model taxing on an emotional level, and perhaps be robbing yourself of the opportunity to start the business you've always dreamed of.

Life After a
PUBLISHING CONTRACT

"And when you live every day with all your heart, then you can be happy ever after." - **The 10th Kingdom**

So, once you sign a contract can you just live happily ever after? Sort of, if you're doing the work you really love. But as ever there are some turns in the path you'd do well to be aware of.

If you make the decision to sign a traditional contract, the process of signing that contract will take much longer then you might expect. Perhaps one of the reasons authors are always so impatient to get their hands on the contract is because they won't feel like the deal is sealed until they do. The other reason is that the advance, or at least the first portion of the advance, is not payable until the publisher receives the signed contract back. This can take a few weeks, especially if your agent is trying to secure more favourable terms.

Once it arrives and you sign it, you should have your money a few weeks after that. Again, no buying that limited edition *Ghostbusters* figurine until the money is showing in your account. Deal?

Once the contract is signed, your relationship with your editor will start to ramp up. When publishers acquire a new author they ask them to fill in an author questionnaire. This will include many questions including your contact details; information about your social media presence; your writing credentials and any other facts about you that the publisher could use to market your work. The first time I ever filled in an author questionnaire, I took a long time over it believing the information would be exploited to promote my work. Er, yes. I was the kid at school who was always asking their English teacher for extra homework. Why do you ask?

Although I'm sure it makes a useful document from time to time, in my general experience, I don't feel as though this information has really been the cornerstone of any publicity or marketing surrounding my books. Consequently, you should do your best to fill in the questionnaire but if obtaining a particular piece of information requires excessive research, or take you a long time to find, I would say there are better uses of your time.

Once all this has been confirmed and sent back to your editor, the editorial process will begin. The editor will complete a developmental edit on your manuscript where they highlight areas of the story that they think need some adjustment. They will likely offer some line editing as well where they feel the wording could be sharper. They will then send this manuscript back to you and you will be expected to act on those changes. You don't have to action every last one of the changes, but you do need to respond to them all so the editor knows you have at least considered their point of view on whatever matter they have raised. If your editor feels strongly about a particular point you don't wish to action there may be additional back and forth about this.

The next stage is the copy-edit. Your work will go off to a third-party copy-editor who will address any final issues with spelling, punctuation, grammar, fact-checking, and if they think there are still elements of the story that don't make sense, they will raise them too. You will then need to fix the final problems and approve the copy editor's changes before the manuscript is sent for its final proof.

A few months before publication you should receive the final proof of the manuscript so you can make any last corrections in the document. You will be given a set deadline for completing this so that the publisher has time to get the finished book off to press in time for the publication date. If you think making final corrections is a small task, you should know that I have spotted upwards of thirty corrections to be made in a 70,000 word manuscript after all of this editing has taken place. It is a very important part of the process and is required to make sure things that were changed during the back and forth of the editorial process make sense.

Any readers who believed signing the contract was the end of the story are probably starting to rethink their perspective. In traditional fairytale terms, signing the contract is the equivalent of the prince marrying the princess. As it turns out, the happily ever after takes a lot more work than you might have anticipated when you were too busy mooning over the glass slippers you bought with your advance money. Even once the book is published your work is not over as you will need to take part in the promotional activities and support any marketing activities arranged by the publisher.

There is no bypassing the editorial process by choosing the independent publishing route either. Well, actually, it's not that you can't publish without an editor, but it is not advisable to do so if you want to create a quality product that will be well-reviewed by readers. Perhaps the slight difference with independent publishing, editorially speaking, is that you have a little bit more freedom to decide which comments you are going to act upon, but you will still need an editorial process.

It's important to hear other people's opinions on your work. If you don't do this you put yourself at risk of hearing about the problems in your book for the first time in an unforgiving Amazon review box from a reviewer who won't sensitively deliver the feedback but will tell the world bluntly what they think of the product you produced. This kind of experience might stop your writing for good so please don't put yourself in that position and recognise that, whether you are independently published or traditionally published, this is a vital process when creating a book.

If you choose the traditional route, you will find that your attitude towards publishing will shift once you've got your second or third book out there. This is because being traditionally published will stop being some far off fantasy on Planet Z (actual planet, the scientists just haven't found it yet) and will become your everyday experience. You will understand firsthand the realities I have discussed in this book and you will realise that having your book published is not necessarily the golden prize you were taught it was, but a method of producing a product in an industry that, just like any other industry, has both positive and difficult aspects to manage.

You will also learn that the army of friends who swore they would buy your book when you published it were not being entirely truthful. I once saw a meme that summed up perfectly what really happens when your book hits the shelves. The meme was split into two shots from *The Lord of the Rings: The Two Towers.* The first shot was the scene where the orc army is waiting to attack Helm's Deep. The caption read: the number of people who say they will buy your book. The second shot pictured just Aragon, Legolas, and Gimli standing next to each other. The caption read: the number of people who will actually buy your book.

To be fair you're not really just trying to sell to your friends and family. That's not the aim of an author who desires wide-reaching impact or one who is trying to build a larger readership, so don't worry about it and don't stress your friends out about it. They are probably just scared of buying your book in case it's bad and they don't want to hurt your feelings when they have to talk to you about it. They don't know it's the best book ever written, they're too scared to find out.

These are just some of the many hurdles you will face once you have been traditionally published. There will also be professional jealousy from others, who will only see your publishing success and not the thousands of hours you put into creating that piece of work and the things you sacrificed to make that happen. You will receive reviews that are frustrating, mean-spirited and generally give you the impression that the reviewer didn't bother to read your book properly.

You will also realise that your mind has played a very mean trick. It will have told you all this time that once you were published, you could sit back and declare: 'I've made it'. That once you were published, you could rest easy because you'd achieved what you set out to achieve. And now you are published, your mind will dispatch a small army of its sneakiest trolls to move the goalposts when you are not looking, because God forbid you ever believe you are a good writer who has accomplished the things you set out to accomplish.

Through all this, I encourage you to keep writing.

Write anything: diary entries, letters, poems, blog posts, flash fiction, your next novel, anything that keeps you umbilically attached to the creative process. Creativity can be an anchor for you in unexpected and tricky times. It can help you remember why you do it when your publisher fails to post to Facebook like they promised. Or when your sales rank takes a sudden dive because apparently people don't want to read about time-travelling pirates anymore. I'm just kidding that will never happen. Everyone wants to read about time-travelling pirates, right? Even if that did happen you can write through it, and, by doing so, you can continue to create new assets to sell and to build your profile. But, most importantly, to develop your own understanding of the craft and your own connection to it.

HYBRID
LIFE

—

Although I've spent most of this book talking about publishing in binary terms; encouraging this gentle reader, who has so loyally stayed with me for more than a hundred pages, to choose between independent publishing and traditional publishing, there is of course a secret third door. Or perhaps a not-so-secret third door given that I told you I'd walked through it at the very beginning of this book.

The third door is the door of the hybrid author, an author who writes both for traditional houses and who chooses to publish independently. This is a best fit for many authors for a number of reasons. Firstly, as hinted at in general throughout this book, authors, and indeed artists of all kinds, would do well to develop as many streams of income as possible in order to achieve financial security. By point blank refusing to engage with either traditional or independent publishing you are closing off one avenue of potential income.

Some might argue that the hybrid route means you have to deal with the worst realities of both publishing routes, which is true, but you also get the best of both routes. Even for their flaws, I love them both and savour every second I get to spend working on these projects. Any business has hard realities. In becoming a hybrid author however, you can access several other perks, besides income, that are unavailable to those who stick to one publishing route. For one thing, being a hybrid author enables you to future-proof your business because if at any point the worst happened and traditional publishing houses were unable to operate or Amazon decided to stop their self-publishing service, you would still have another avenue available to you for putting your work out into the world and generating income from it. For instance, in the middle of a global pandemic when all the traditional bookshops have sadly closed their doors, you could write something new — as I have done with this book — and put it out into the world to help others or generate much-needed income.

Now, OK, I concede that these are extraordinary circumstances not likely to happen every day but if one thing can affect the book business in the way Covid-19 has, then there are likely to be other things out there that can do the same. Protecting your business, giving yourself the chance to remain creative and continue to generate income in difficult times is just good common sense.

Being a hybrid author also keeps you up-to-date in all aspects of your business. You will learn from the expertise of publishers who have regular briefings for all staff to share knowledge in the industry and who spend their time looking for ways to sell more books. You will also spend time on personal and professional development so that you can effectively sell the books you have self-published. Thus, any conversations you have with your publisher or editor will come from a more informed standpoint.

Becoming a hybrid author also allows you some freedom and flexibility, especially if you are interested in writing under a range of pen names, so you can explore different genres, different kinds of stories and collaborate with other high-profile independent authors. Otherwise, you are likely to spend a lot of your time writing only what your publishing contract states you should write. For some writers this can feel too restrictive over time.

Of course, in order to self-publish you need to ensure you are not in breach of your publishing contract. This is just one of the reasons why it is so important to ask your agent to pay close attention to the option clause and keep it as narrow as possible. This way, will be able to write in other genres and other formats without nullifying the agreement you made with the publisher. If you are considering writing in other genres or formats on an independent basis, you will also need to ensure you are not in breach of the contract you signed with your agent. Technically speaking, they should have first refusal on all manuscripts that you produce because they might be able to sell that manuscript and receive a commission from your work.

I have had the good fortune of signing with the best agent available on the planet, one who understands an author's need for a portfolio income and also understands that the landscape of publishing is changing fast. Thus, we have an agreement that allows me to independently publish shorter works that I might be able to get a bit of pin money for along the way.

Before you sign an agreement with any agent it is worth knowing what their stance is on your right to publish works on your own steam. If they are unwilling to let you do this under any circumstances, you may want to think twice about signing a contract with that particular agent whilst the publishing industry is in such a state of flux. Writers need flexibility to be able to maximise their income and profile-building opportunities. As previously outlined in this book, traditional publishers are not always guaranteed to say yes to a manuscript. Thus, it's important to know what other options are available to you should this situation present itself.

The final reason I think it's a great idea to be an hybrid author is because it helps you work with traditional editors. Once you have put a book together that you are entirely responsible for, you will know what it really takes to make that happen. This will no doubt inspire a newfound empathy for your editor and the work that they do. This is difficult to otherwise achieve, so being a hybrid author will not only help you maximize your income but actually help you navigate traditional publishing deals and relationships with more confidence and understanding.

ON THE 'WHEN'

—

This volume has examined the 'how' and the 'when' of signing book deals at length, but I wanted to offer one final say on the 'when.' In my opinion, you should only sign a book deal when you are satisfied that the other parties involved are invested in your work; will keep their word about how much they will promote it; and when the contract does not prohibit you from pursuing other creative avenues that may be lucrative or beneficial to your craft as a writer.

If you are one of the many writers who wants a traditional contract so they can focus solely on writing, please be aware that some marketing will still be required if the publisher does not succeed in raising the profile of your book on their own. If you are prepared for this eventuality and, if having read about the realities of a traditional contract in this book you still want to sign that contract, then by all means dig your best pen out and put it in writing.

As I hope I have underlined in this volume, there is no one easy path through publishing. Each path has its own dragons and quagmires. The trick is to take a good, long look at the adventure map so that you are forewarned and forearmed before you set out on this quest.

Every time a review is left for this book a dragon gets his wings.

RESOURCES

___

BOOKS	
How to Write a Sizzling Synopsis	Bryan Cohen
Bird by Bird	Anne Lamott
Become a Successful Indie Author	Craig Martelle
Successful Self-Publishing	Joanna Penn
Amazon Ads Unleashed	Robert J. Ryan

WEBSITES	
Alliance of Independent Authors	allianceindependentauthors.org
Kindlepreneur	kindlepreneur.com
K-lytics	k-lytics.com
Kobo Writing Life Podcast	kobowritinglife.com
Self-Publishing Formula	selfpublishingformula.com

| The Creative Penn | thecreativepenn.com |

You can also access a creative writing starter library including a Publishing Masterplan, Character Creation Masterplan and World-Building Masterplan by signing up to my writers community email list at:

helencoxbooks.com/writerscommunitylist

ACKNOWLEDGMENTS

It is impossible to acknowledge absolutely every person who made the writing of this book possible. It is the culmination of many experiences with a variety of personalities over the past decade in publishing.

But let me thank my agent, Joanna Swainson for being there through every twist my writing journey has taken. Thanks also to Quercus Books, the publisher who continues to say 'yes' to my somewhat zany output and who are, in my opinion, leading the way with the author experience.

Gratitude also to my editor and proof reader J Mills, and to the many students at City Lit who asked me to write this book in the first place. I hope it's useful to you, and I wish you luck and great fortune with your writing and all else.